Growing Up in God's Word

Bible Curriculum

"... from childhood you have known the Holy Scriptures..."
(2 Timothy 3:15, NKJV)

GENESIS

Cover illustration: The Garden of Eden by Jan Brueghel, the Elder, 1612 Public Domain Image

Written and illustrated by Heather M. Pryor

Table of Contents

Introduction

Why teach children the Bible using only the Bible? Can they understand it? Yes! Is it too boring? No! I have taught a children's Bible class on Sunday mornings for over twenty years and have home-schooled my three children, teaching them the Bible in our home. Guess what? Children are a lot smarter than we give them credit for! There are just a few key things to remember in teaching the Bible to children. First, we need to be enthusiastic about the Bible ourselves. If children see that we think the Bible is boring, they will most likely adopt the same opinion. Be excited about opening the word of God together! Second, don't be afraid to tell them you don't know know an answer to their question. There are many things in the Bible that we have questions about; some things we are able to study and find an answer for, others will have to wait until we get to heaven and can ask God. It's okay to let them know you're stumped too, but encourage them to search for the answer with you. Third, set the bar high for them. Please, please, please don't "dumb" the Bible down to "their level". Children can understand a lot through patient explanation and teaching. For example, if you read a hard word in the Bible that they may not be familiar with, stop and ask them what they think it means, then give them a correct definition. Now they have learned a new word and understand the passage you've just read at the same time. Children like to be challenged and to meet our expectations for them.

The method in this curriculum works because it has been tried among many children of different ages, abilities and levels. Here is the best proof I can offer to you: One of my regular Sunday morning students brought a friend to our class one day. She answered a few questions but mostly sat very quietly, absorbing everything that was going on. Later on, the woman that brought her to church said that the little girl told them on the way home that she wanted to come to our Sunday school class every week because we *actually teach from the Bible*. This little girl is not "unchurched" by any means; in fact, she regularly attends a denominational megachurch every Sunday. As the scripture says, "Out of the mouths of babes!"

May your children be like Timothy in the Bible who, *"from childhood has known the holy Scriptures"* (II Timothy 3:15), and may God bless you as you study His word together.

How to Use this Curriculum

Life began in a garden, so we will be using garden references and symbols throughout this curriculum to designate the different activities. Luke 8:11 says that *"the seed is the word of God"*. Our hearts are the soil that the seed needs to be planted in. We should desire to cultivate the soil of our hearts and the hearts of our children to receive the word so that it will grow and produce good fruit for our Lord.

"Growing In The Word": Lesson Text And Discussion

This is the most important part of the curriculum – the teaching of God's Word. The lesson text is broken down into manageable sections to be read aloud and then discussed. If children are old enough to read, let them read out loud. If there are several verses to be read as a section, you could take turns reading a couple of verses per person. If it helps your child, let them jot down notes or write down definitions to new words as you discuss the passage. Encourage them to ask questions and ask them leading questions to get them thinking. The discussion section is basically a paraphrasing of what was just read to make sure there is comprehension of the material. Frequently there are questions to be answered during the discussion phase as well. The section of verses often leave off at a "cliffhanger" moment which helps keep the children engaged. You read and discuss and then you're ready to read on to see what happens next. At the end of this section of the curriculum there are review questions. These can be used in several ways: You may ask them at the end of the lesson, at the end of the week for a review, or if you want to have a graded assignment, you can use them as an oral or written quiz.

*A word about translations. It is important to use a reliable and accurate translation. Some dependable ones are KJV, NKJV, ESV and ASV (American Standard). Many modern translations have compromised the integrity of the Scriptures in trying to put it in "easier to understand" language. All references in this curriculum are taken from the New King James Version.

"Putting Down Roots": Memory Work

Memory work should be practiced every day for the entire week. Use whatever method works the best according to your child's learning style. Here is a link with a list of aids for memorizing scripture: http://pryorconvictions.com/memorizing-scripture/ The Psalmist said in Psalm 119:11, *"Thy word have I hid in my heart that I might not sin against Thee."* I cannot stress enough how important it is to memorize Scripture. In addition to Scripture, sometimes there are other items included in the Memory Work such as lists of things or categories. A challenge to parents: memorize it with your children!

"Farther Afield": Map Work

There are blank maps provided in Appendix A in the back of the book. These may be photocopied for home use with this curriculum. Most lessons have mapping activities to serve as a visual aid of the places you read about in scripture. To be consistent, you may want to follow a system such as: cities – red, countries – green, bodies of water – blue, wilderness or desert areas – brown, lands or regions – yellow. The map work will indicate different places to be located on the map. Locate and label each item.

"Harvest Fun": Games And Activities

There are games and activities for each lesson to help review and reinforce the material that was covered. It is best to read through these at the beginning of the week to see if any planning ahead needs to be done.

"Digging Deeper": Research

This is primarily for the older students who are able to work independently. If your younger children wish to do these assignments with your help, then by all means, let them! It is a good idea to keep a notebook for these written assignments. These assignments are meant to encourage students of the Bible to learn how to study a topic deeper by using other resources to shed light on the subject. Primarily, books and the Internet will be your sources of information so it's important to do two things: 1) Check the reliability of your source, and 2) Check multiple sources; you might find two or more very different theories or opinions. Some good resources to use are Bible commentaries, concordances (such as Strong's), Bible dictionaries, Bible atlases and Bible software. There are many things we run across in the Bible that we would like to know more about. Have fun exploring!

"Food For Thought": Puzzles

There are at least two puzzles with each lesson to, again, provide review and reinforcement or plain just to have fun! The puzzles may be worked in the book or photocopied. All puzzle answers are provided in the Answer Key in the back of the book.

"Fruits Of Our Labor": Crafts

There are at least two crafts to do with each lesson. They vary in level of difficulty, but are another means of reinforcement of material covered. Crafts are a good activity for the kinesthetic (hands-on) learner as well as a tangible reminder for the visual learner. Please read ahead early in the week to see what materials you may need to gather in advance.

Suggested Schedule

This curriculum is designed to be used five days a week, 30 minutes to 1 hour per day. It is designed to be used with multiple ages with some activities geared toward older children and others geared toward younger. You may use as much or as little of the activities listed as you choose. Please feel free to alter the suggested schedule to fit the time constraints and needs of your family. However, the lesson and memory work portions should be used for all ages.

Begin or end each day's activities with prayer.

- Day 1 – Read "Growing in the Word":Lesson Text and Discussion. Begin "Putting Down Roots": Memory Work assignments.

- Day 2 – Continue memory work, do "Farther Afield": Map Work activities, and "Harvest Fun": Games and Activities.

- Day 3 – Continue memory work, do "Digging Deeper":Research activities, and/or "Food for Thought": Puzzles.

- Day 4 – Continue memory work, do "Fruits of Our Labor": Crafts, or continue working on previous activities.

- Day 5 – Recite memory work, do lesson Review Questions and finish any assignments or activities from the week that time didn't permit.

Lesson 1: Creation

Text: Genesis 1 & 2

"Growing In The Word": Lesson Text & Discussion

Read Genesis 1:1-5. God was the powerful Creator who was there before the world was ever created. He brought everything into being just by His spoken word! Count the number of times it says in chapter 1, "Then God *said*..." In the very first verse of the Bible, we see the five elements of the universe: **time** (In the beginning), **force** (God), **energy** (created), **space** (the heavens), and **matter** (and the earth). The first recorded words of God are, *"Let there be light."* What did God call the light? (Day) What did God call the darkness? (Night) On the first day of creation, God created light.

Read Genesis 1:6-8. These verses talk about dividing the waters. What does that mean? The water on the earth is found in places like our oceans, seas, and rivers, but there is water in the air as well. If you have ever studied the water cycle in school, you learned about how sunlight evaporates water on the earth. The water doesn't just disappear but is stored in the clouds. When the clouds get too full of water, we have rain and the water falls back to earth again. God separated the waters on the earth from the waters in the sky with a firmament that he stretched out all the way around the earth. The firmament is the atmosphere or the air we breathe. The firmament was called "the heavens". We often refer to it as the sky. On the second day of creation, God created the firmament or air we breathe.

Read Genesis 1:9-13. Notice that every tree and herb and plant were to bring forth fruit and seeds according to its own kind. That means an apple tree wouldn't bear pears, a pear tree would bear pears, and you wouldn't see a cucumber plant growing green beans! How does God start referring to His creation? (He calls it good.) On the third day of creation, God created the dry land and all vegetation (green things!).

Read Genesis 1:14-19. What were the reasons God made the sun, moon, and stars? (Day and night, signs and seasons, days and years, and for light.) The greater light was the _(sun)_ and it was to shine in the day, and the lesser light was the _(moon)_ which was to shine at night. On the fourth day of creation, God created the sun, moon, and the stars.

Read Genesis 1:20-23. On the fifth day, God created every creature that lives in the seas and that flies in the skies. This would include flying dinosaurs like the pteradactyls and the mighty leviathan (which lived in the water) that we read about in Job chapter 41 and Psalm 104:25, 26. Also included on this day would be anything with wings such as bats and even insects. An easy way to remember this day is: Fish and Fowl on day Five.

Read Genesis 1:24-25. Day six saw God creating all of the land animals – even the dinosaurs. All of the animals were to reproduce after their own kind, just like the plants. In other words, giraffes had baby giraffes – not baby rhinos!

Read Genesis 1:26. God was not alone during the creation process. Notice that He uses the pronouns "Us" and "Our". Who was with Him? God is in three persons: God the Father, God the Son (Jesus), and God the Holy Spirit. You might have heard this called the Trinity or the Godhead. God was going to make man in His own image and let man have dominion (or authority) over all living things on the earth. The animals were not created equal to man, rather, man was created to be superior to or over all other living things on the earth.

Read Genesis 1:27-28. Man and woman were also created on the sixth day, but we don't read about the details of how they were created until we get to chapter 2. God commands them to *"be fruitful and multiply"* which means, have children! He wants people to multiply and fill the earth and man will have dominion over all of the animals and birds and fish.

Read Genesis 1:29-30. What did God instruct man, woman, and animals to eat? (Vegetation – no meat-eating yet!)

Read Genesis 1:31. God saw everything He had created and declared it to be <u>very</u> good. His creation was perfection.

Read Genesis 2:1-3. God created the universe, the world, and everything in it in six literal twenty-four hour days. What did He do on the seventh day? (He rested.) This did not mean He was tired, but rather He had finished His work. God blessed this seventh day and sanctified it. What does sanctified mean? (Set apart)

Read Genesis 2:4-6. In the very beginning, before the flood of Noah, there was no rain on the earth. So, how did the plants grow? (God caused a mist to come up from the ground to water the earth.)

Read Genesis 2:7. This verse tells us *how* God made man back in chapter 1, verse 27. What was man formed from? (The dust of the earth) God formed man out of the dust of the earth and breathed the breath of life into him.

Read Genesis 2:8-14. God provided everything for man including a perfect and beautiful first home, the garden of Eden. What was located in the middle of this garden? (The tree of life and the tree of the knowledge of good and evil.) A river also flowed through the garden of Eden and split into 4 separate riverheads. What were the names of these 4 rivers? (Pishon, Gihon, Hiddekel, Euphrates)

Read Genesis 2:15-17. God gave the man work to do. It was not back-breaking work by any means, but it was a job that gave him responsibility and something productive to do each day. What was his job? (To look after or tend the garden and to keep it) God told the man that every tree that was created was provided to him for food...except just one. Which tree was forbidden to man and why? (The tree of the knowledge of good and evil was forbidden. If he ate of it, he would die.) God had given man everything he needed and could want. The creation was beautiful and satisfying. This one tree was placed in the garden and forbidden because God has always given man a choice. Man can choose to obey the Lord, or he will choose to disobey Him.

Read Genesis 2:18-20. These events are taking place on the sixth day of creation when the Lord created man, woman, and all of the land animals. They are just being explained in more detail in this chapter. As God was in the process of creating everything, He kept referring to His creation as good. What does He see that is *not* good? (The fact that man is alone.) God knows that Adam needs someone who is suitable for him, but He wants Adam to realize it too. God gives Adam another job to do. What is it? (Naming the animals) Would you have liked this job? Adam must have been pretty creative to think up all of those wonderful names of animals! As animal after animal walks by him to receive its name, what does Adam realize? (None of these animals would make a proper partner for me!)

Read Genesis 2:21-22. Describe the process of God's creation of woman. (God made Adam fall into a deep sleep, then He opened up Adam's side and removed one of his ribs. God closed up Adam's side, then formed woman from the rib taken from Adam.) God performed the first surgery ever!

Read Genesis 2:23-25. What was Adam's reaction to the woman whom God created for him? (He was excited!) Why did Adam say she would be called a woman? (Because she was taken out of man) God not only performed the first surgery ever, He also performed the first wedding ceremony. He brought the woman to the man so the two of them could be joined together as one. From the beginning of time, God provided marriage to be a beautiful union between one man and one woman.

Genesis chapter 1 and chapter 2 give us the wonderful account of how our mighty God brought everything there is into existence. Praise Him for His wondrous works!

<u>Review Questions</u>:   (Answers are provided in the Answer Key.)

1. Who was in the beginning before creation?

2. What five elements do we see in the very first verse of the Bible?

3. What did God create on each of the seven days?

4. What does it mean for plants, trees, and animals to bring forth "after their own kind"?

5. What were some of the reasons God made the sun, moon and stars?

6. Who are the "3 persons" of God?

7. After everything was created, how did God describe it?

8. What did God give man authority over?

9. What watered the earth when there was no rain?

10. What did God make man out of?

11. Did God create dinosaurs?   Did they live with man?   How do we know?

12. Describe the creation of man.

13. Described the creation of the woman.

14. What 4 rivers flowed out of the garden of Eden?

15. What one tree was forbidden to man by God?

 "Putting Down Roots": Memory Work

• Memorize Genesis 1:1

• Memorize Genesis 2:24

• Memorize the 7 days of creation: Day 1-light, Day 2-firmament or air we breathe,

Day 3-dry land and green things, Day 4-sun, moon and stars, Day 5-fish and fowl, Day 6-man, woman, and land animals, Day 7-God rested

 ## "Farther Afield": Map Work

Map 1

- Locate Mesopotamia

- Locate the Garden of Eden. Hmmm...We don't know its exact location, but the Bible gives us a few clues. Genesis 2:8 - it was in the east. Genesis 2:11 - a river and land we don't know. Genesis 2:13 - a river and land we don't know. Genesis 2:14 - two rivers, one we know and a country we know. Our best guess would be somewhere in modern day Iraq.

- Locate the river Euphrates

- Locate the country of Assyria

 ## "Harvest Fun": Games & Activities

- Creation Scavenger Hunt - Make a list of items found in nature and see how many you can find. To liven things up, set a timer to see who can find the most items on the list in the time given. Try to choose items from as many of the days of creation as possible. To challenge older students, have them look up and write the Latin name of identification for each of the items on the list.

- Creation Memory Game - Make pairs of cards with matching pictures of anything in nature (2 leaves, 2 mountains, 2 fish, etc.) or use the Creation Cards in Appendix B. You may want to back these with construction paper so they won't be see-through. Mix up the cards and place them face down on a table. Take turns picking two cards at a time, trying to make a match. As matches are found, make it more challenging by asking on what day of creation it was made.

- Zoo Field Trip - This would be a fun location to do a scavenger hunt too!

"Digging Deeper": Research

- Adam - How long did he live? (Genesis 5:5) What body part did God use from him to make woman? (Genesis 2:22) What job did God give him in Genesis 2:19-20? What did he name his first three sons? (Genesis 4:1, 2, 25)

- Photosynthesis - Read about "photosynthesis" and why it is necessary for plants to grow. Now, what day did God create all plant life? (Day 3) What day did He create the sun? (Day 4) How does this help prove that evolution *couldn't* have happened?

- Dinosaurs - There are lots of resources on dinosaurs, but many of them are from an evolutionist viewpoint. Here are some recommended books from a creationist point of view to help you with your research: *Dinosaurs Unleashed* by Kyle Butt and Eric Lyons, *Jurassic Park v. Jehovah's Park* by Catie Frates, and *Dinosaurs by Design* by Duane T. Gish. Job chapters 40 and 41 both refer to dinosaurs but by different names. What names are given? So, why isn't the word "dinosaur" in the Bible? Find out what year the word was invented and who came up with it.

 ## "Food For Thought": Puzzles

- Coded Message:

__ __ __   __ __ __ __ __ __ __   __ __ __
20 12 23   24 9 22 26 7 22 23   7 19 22

__ __ __ __ __ __ __ __   __ __ __
6 13 18 5 22 9 8 22   26 13 23

__ __ __ __ __ __ __ __ __ __   __ __   __ __   __ __
22 5 22 9 2 7 19 18 13 20   18 13   18 7   25 2

__ __ __   __ __ __ __ __ __   __ __ __ __ .
19 18 8   8 11 12 16 22 13   4 12 9 23

<u>Key to the Code</u>:

F	N	R	U	A	G	O	S	V	C	H	T	D	I	E	B	W	K	Y	P	M	L
21	13	9	6	26	20	12	8	5	24	19	7	23	18	22	25	4	16	2	11	14	15

- Word Scramble - Unscramble the following words using the clues to help you. Answers are provided in the Answer Key.

When did God create the heavens and the earth?   nngbiengi _____

What did God call the firmament?   enhvae _____

What did God make in His image?   nma _____

What did God do on the seventh day?   esdtre _____

What watered the face of the earth?   mtsi _____

What did God form man out of?   Stud _____

"Fruits Of Our Labor": Crafts

- Creation mural or creation mobile - To make a mural, take a large piece of poster board or butcher paper. Draw or paint a creation scene that includes something from each day of creation. To make a mobile, use a wire coat hanger, several pieces of string or yarn, and some card stock. Draw small pictures of different items from each of the days of creation, cut them out, tape a piece of string or yarn to the back and then tie onto the hanger. Make the pieces of string or yarn different lengths so you can fit more on your mobile. When finished, hang your mobile where you can see it and enjoy it.

- Terrarium - Remember we learned that before the flood there was no rain? In the beginning, the climate of the earth was very tropical – warm and moist. Make a terrarium to help demonstrate the environment in the Garden of Eden. You will need an empty plastic 2 liter bottle, 3-5 small plants, potting soil, and some gravel or small stones. First, measure about six inches up on the bottle and draw a line. Carefully cut the bottle all the way through at this line. Put a one-inch layer of stones in the bottom of your bottle, then fill the bottle with soil to within about an inch of the rim. Arrange your plants in the soil then water them. Place the top part of the soda bottle back onto the bottom pushing it down over the bottom part. Place the bottle in a warm, sunny location.

Lesson 2: Sin Enters the World

Text: Genesis 3

"Growing In The Word": Lesson Text & Discussion

Read Genesis 3:1. The serpent is Satan and he approaches Eve to deceive her. What does "deceive" mean? (To lie to; to trick.) John 8:44 tells us that Satan is a liar and the father of lies. He starts off by lying to Eve about what God said. God did *not* say they couldn't eat of any tree of the garden. In fact, in Genesis 2:16 He told them that they were to eat freely of every tree in the garden except just one! What was the name of this tree? (The tree of the knowledge of good and evil)

Read Genesis 3:2-3. Does Eve accurately quote God? Read Genesis 2:16-17 to find out.

Read Genesis 3:4-5. Satan is calling God a liar! He's telling Eve, 1) You *won't* die, and 2) God's just "afraid" you'll be like Him if you eat this fruit.

Read Genesis 3:6. Eve gives in to the three basic temptations that Satan uses on all mankind:

- *Lust of the flesh - "good for food"
- Lust of the eyes - "a delight to the eyes"
- Pride of life - "make one wise"

*Lust – an unlawful or wrong desire

I John 2:16 speaks of these three temptations. Eve then involves her husband Adam in her sin. Adam submits to his wife and eats the forbidden fruit. Sadly, this is backwards. In **Ephesians 5:25** it says that wives are to submit to their husbands, not the other way around. You might wonder why they didn't die like God said they would. First of all, before they sinned, they were immortal which means they would never have experienced physical death. When they ate of the fruit, their bodies began from that moment to grow older and approach a day of physical death. They lived for hundreds of years after this, but they did eventually die a physical death. Second, they died spiritually. That is, they no longer had a perfect relationship with God but were now separated from Him by their sin. God did not lie – He never does!

Read Genesis 3:7. This is one big OOPS! moment. They didn't get the thrill they were looking for about how lofty and wise they would now be. Instead, their eyes are "opened" to how things *really* are and what a terrible thing they've done and they are ashamed. We sometimes fall into the same trap. We want to do something soooo bad that we know we shouldn't, but we give in and do it anyway. It doesn't take very long for the good feeling to be gone and the bad feeling of "Oh No!" to set in. Adam and Eve had been naked since their creation, there was no shame in it. Now that sin has entered the world, they are ashamed of being naked and want to cover themselves. What do they try to use to cover themselves? (Fig leaves)

Read Genesis 3:8. Adam and Eve hear God walking in the garden and try to hide in their disgrace. Sin separates us from God. Adam and Eve no longer have the same open and close relationship with God that they had before. Sin has now come between them.

Read Genesis 3:9-11. What question does God ask Adam and Eve? *("Where are you?")*

Does God really not know where they are or what they had done? Of course He did! He asks them this question to get them to realize the seriousness of what they had done.

Read Genesis 3:12. Who does Adam blame? (Eve and also God because He gave the woman to Adam.)

Read Genesis 3:13. Who does Eve blame? (The serpent for deceiving her) Does blaming someone else excuse you of the wrong you've done? (No) When we have done something wrong, God wants us to confess or admit the sin and take responsibility for it, not blame someone else.

Read Genesis 3:14. How does God curse the serpent? (It is cursed above all animals and will have to crawl on its belly and eat dust.)

Read Genesis 3:15. This is the "mother promise" of the entire Bible. It is the first prophecy of the coming Savior, Jesus Christ. Satan would deal a temporary, but not deadly blow to Jesus by the crucifixion (bruise his heel), but Christ's power over death and the grave through His resurrection would be fatal to Satan (bruise his head). God gives man hope and a promise of salvation from the very beginning.

Read Genesis 3:16. How was woman cursed? (She will have pain in childbirth, and her husband will rule over her.)

Read Genesis 3:17-19. How was man cursed? (He will have to use hard labor and sweat to bring forth food from the ground, and he will die a physical death [dust to dust].)

Read Genesis 3:20. Adam officially gives his wife a name. What does "Eve" mean? (Mother of all living)

Read Genesis 3:21. Who made Adam and Eve's clothes? (God) What were the clothes made from? (Animal skins) This required a sacrifice (death).

Read Genesis 3:22. Who is the "Us"? Remember from our last lesson? (Father, Son, and Holy Spirit) What would happen if Adam and Eve ate of the tree of life? They would be immortal (again!). The Lord does not want this and will not allow it to happen.

Read Genesis 3:23. What was Adam to do now after being sent out of the garden? (Work the ground.)

Read Genesis 3:24. What did God do to make sure they didn't return to the garden to try to eat of the tree of life? (He placed a cherubim and flaming sword as a guard.) What a sad ending to such a happy beginning! However, remember that God doesn't leave them hopeless. They have the promise of a coming Savior - Jesus Christ the Lord!

Review Questions: (Answers are provided in the Answer Key.)

1. Who was the serpent?

2. What is Satan the father of?

3. How many trees were Adam and Eve not allowed to eat of?

4. What was it called?

5. What lie did Satan tell Eve regarding eating the fruit?

6. What three temptations did Eve give in to?

7. What did Adam and Eve try to sew together to make clothes?

8. Whom did they try to hide from?

9. Whom did Adam blame?

10. Whom did Eve blame?

11. How was the serpent cursed?

12. What is the "mother promise" of the Bible?

13. Whom does Genesis 3:15 prophecy about?

14. How was the woman cursed?

15. How was the man cursed?

16. What does "Eve" mean?

17. From what did God make clothes for Adam and Eve?

18. What tree did God not want Adam and Eve to eat of after they'd sinned?

19. What did God do to keep them from returning to Eden and eating of this tree?

20. What kind of fruit did Adam and Eve eat?

 ## "Putting Down Roots": Memory Work

- Memorize Genesis 3:15

 ## "Farther Afield": Map Work

Map 1

- Locate the country of Iraq – This is possibly the general area where the garden of Eden was located. On the east side of it, draw a cherubim (angel) with a flaming sword or place an angel sticker.

"Harvest Fun": Games & Activities

- "Stay Away from Satan!" - Use the cards from Lesson 1's Memory Game. Make four new cards with the word "Satan" written in black. Shuffle all of the cards and deal five to each player. Have a draw pile and discard pile. (Play this game similar to Old Maid.) Let each player lay down their matches. If someone is holding a "Satan" card or draws one, they immediately lay it down yelling, "Stay away from Satan!" Whoever has the most matches wins the game. Stress the importance of not letting Satan get close enough to tempt us. This game would also provide a good opportunity to review what day of creation each item was made.

- Hide and Seek – Play an old-fashioned game of Hide and Seek. Discuss how Adam and Eve tried to hide from God, but it didn't work. He knew **exactly** where they were (and what they'd done!). Explain that God sees all we do – there is no hiding from Him. Read Jeremiah 23:24.

"Digging Deeper": Research

- Cherubim - What is a cherubim? How does the Bible describe them? How many times is the word "cherubim" used in the Bible? Draw a picture of what you think they looked like based on what you learn.

- Satan - What was Satan? (not the serpent, but something else) Where did he used to be? What happened to him? What does the name "Satan" mean?

 ## "Food For Thought": Puzzles

- Word Search – On the following page is a word search puzzle containing various words from this lesson. The answers are provided in the Answer Key. Happy hunting!

```
C D S U D N A R S M A D A H C
R R U I I E D D N P E E E E U
T O L S E S V C E E N V V E R
A W T O T C H E R U B I M L S
E S I U R B K N O W L E D G E
W E U R E D I E P S E C L E D
S P R U E A R S E R P E N T O
E U F U P D O O G A R D E N K
```

serpent	garden	fruit	knowledge
good	evil	Lord	seed
deceived	heel	bruise	pain
cursed	dust	Adam	Eve
cherubim	sword	tree	sweat
sin			

- Matching – Draw a line from the word on the left to what it matches on the right. Answers are provided in the Answer Key.

Eve	deceiver
serpent	garden
Eden	fig leaves
cherubim	redeemer
covering	mother of all living
Christ	angel
Adam	Lord
garden guard	Satan
heel bruiser	sweating farmer
garden walker	flaming sword

"Fruits Of Our Labor": Crafts

- Flaming sword – Cut a sword shape out of a large piece of sturdy cardboard. Paint it silver or cover it with aluminum foil. Glue or tape strips of orange and yellow tissue paper all around the edges of the blade. Wave your sword back and forth to make "flames"!

- Tree of Knowledge of Good and Evil – Use modeling clay to form a tree of the knowledge of good and evil. Make the fruit very colorful and appealing. Remember Eve thought it looked good enough to eat and sadly, she did.

- Before and After – Draw or paint a picture of life for Adam and Eve before sin entered the world and what life was like after they sinned. Things were very different!

Lesson 3: Cain and Abel

Text: Genesis 4

 ## "Growing In The Word": Lesson Text & Discussion

Read Genesis 4:1-2. Cain was the firstborn son of Adam and Eve, Abel was the second. What were their occupations? (Cain-farmer, Abel-shepherd)

Read Genesis 4:3-5. What did each of them sacrifice to God? (Cain offered of the fruit of the ground; Abel offered animals from his flock.) Whose offering was rejected; whose was respected, and why? (Abel's was accepted; Cain's was rejected.) In **Hebrews 11:4** we read that Abel offered his sacrifice by **faith. Romans 10:17** tells us that, *"Faith comes by hearing and hearing by the word of God"*. So, we can conclude that Abel heard what God wanted them to sacrifice and how it was to be done, then obeyed God completely in faith. What is Cain's reaction to all of this? (He was very angry.)

Read Genesis 4:6-7. God is trying to warn Cain before he does something he'll regret. He warns Cain that sin lies at his door just waiting for him. He's also pointing out to Cain that he shouldn't be surprised at God's rejection of his offering, and therefore, he has no reason to be angry. If Cain had done well (obeyed God completely) then his offering would have been acceptable too. There's a couple of lessons we can learn from this passage: 1) When we get angry, cool down and think clearly before acting, and 2) Obey God completely and do our best. Don't try to do a half-hearted job or do something differently than we're told and expect it to be "good enough".

Read Genesis 4:8. The first murder in the world has now been committed – by one brother to another and all because of jealousy. **Read I John 3:12.** Why does the Bible say Cain killed his brother Abel? (Cain's deeds were evil while Abel's were righteous.)

Read Genesis 4:9. God asks Cain where Abel is. Doesn't He know? Absolutely! But He wants Cain to tell him what he's done. (Remember Adam and Eve hiding after they'd sinned?) God is saying, yes, you are your brother's keeper. Cain lies to God and says he doesn't know where Abel is.

Read Genesis 4:10-12. What does God say is crying out to Him from the ground? (Abel's blood) Abel was murdered, innocent blood was shed, and now justice must be done. God is the judge and He is going to sentence Cain for this crime. God tells Cain what his punishment is to be, and it is great. He is being cast out from the presence of the Lord. Sin is the great separator between God and us. Cain will also now struggle to raise crops from the earth. Remember, his occupation so far in life has been a farmer. God also tells Cain that he will be a fugitive and a vagabond. What do you think those words mean? A fugitive is someone who is on the run trying to escape from a crime he has committed. A vagabond is a wanderer; someone who has no real home.

Read Genesis 4:13-15. Did Cain accept his punishment? (No) What did he think would happen to him? He is worried about his own skin! He is afraid someone will try to kill him for revenge. What did God do to Cain to prevent someone killing him? (God put a special mark on him.) Do we see any sign at all from Cain that he is sorry for what he's done? (No!) Sadly, we see no repentance. Do you know what repentance is? It is much more than just being sorry. It is being so sorry for what you've done that you never want to do it again. You have been going one direction and you stop and go the other way. You change your life by changing your heart. Cain is sorry – sorry he's being punished, but that is all. What Cain is experiencing is called worldly sorrow. It is a sorrow that you got caught and are suffering painful consequences, but it is not a godly sorrow that leads to repentance. **Read II Corinthians 7:10.**

Read Genesis 4:16-17. Where did Cain go and whom did he marry? There's been a lot of speculation as to where Cain got his wife. Notice the Bible does not say Cain went to the land of Nod and *found* a wife. He took her there and she was most likely his sister. Early on, people would have had to marry siblings to multiply and fill the earth. It was allowed by God initially. What was the name of Cain's firstborn son? (Enoch)

Read Genesis 4:18-22. Here we start to see some of the effects of the ungodliness of Cain on his descendants. His great, great, great grandson, Lamech, was the first polygamist in the Bible. What is a polygamist? It is someone who has more than one wife. This was **not** how God designed marriage to be. Notice some of the talents and occupations these men had. Some of them were herdsmen and knew how to successfully breed and manage large herds of animals. Some of them had talent in metal working, making things with bronze and iron. Some of them were talented musicians playing handmade instruments such as the flute and harp. Early men were not some cave-dwelling grunters but intelligent, talented, and able men as God created them to be. Who was known as the father of those who are tent-dwellers with livestock? (Jabal) Who was known as the father of the musicians? (Jubal) Who was a teacher of metalworking? (Tubal-Cain)

Read Genesis 4:23-24. Cain was the first murderer and now we see just a few generations later, another one. Who is mentioned in the Bible as the next murderer? (Lamech) Lamech brags to his wives about the two men he's killed. Who were his two wives? (Adah and Zillah)

Read Genesis 4:25-26. Adam and Eve must have been very sorrowful over their son Cain's sin and banishment, as well as the death of their son, Abel. However, they have a son named Seth who will be a faithful, godly man like Abel had been. Remember Genesis 3:15? Satan knows that God had promised a Savior would come into the world and that Savior would deal him a fatal blow. Satan wants more than anything to prevent this from happening so he will constantly try throughout the Bible to destroy the good "seed line" to prevent the Savior from being born. Having Cain kill Abel was Satan's first attempt, but this does not stop God's promise – the Savior DOES come!

Review Questions: (Answers are provided in the Answer Key.)

1. Who was Adam and Eve's firstborn?

2. What did his name mean?

3. Who was their second born son?

4. What job did Abel have?

5. What job did Cain have?

6. What did Cain bring as an offering?

7. What did Abel bring as an offering?

8. Whose offering was accepted and why?

9. What was Cain's reaction?

10. What did God warn Cain would lie at his door if he didn't do right?

11. What did Cain do to Abel?

12. When God asked Cain where Abel was, what did Cain do?

13. What did God say cried out to him from the ground?

14. What was Cain's punishment?

15. Did Cain take his punishment well?

16. What was he afraid someone would do to him?

17. How did God prevent that?

18. Where did Cain go?

19. Who was his first son?

20. Who took two wives?

21. Who was the father of tent-dwellers?

22. Who was the father of musicians?

23. Who was an instructor of every craftsman in bronze and iron?

24. Who was another murderer besides Cain?

25. Who was the third son of Adam and Eve?

 ## "Putting Down Roots": Memory Work

- Memorize Genesis 4:7

- Memorize II Corinthians 7:10

- Memorize the ungodly line of Cain: Cain-Enoch-Irad-Mehujael-Methushael-Lamech (two wives)-Jabal, Jubal & Tubal-Cain

"Farther Afield": Map Work

Map 1

- Find the angel on your map from Lesson 2. Continue a short distance east from the angel and label it "Nod". Place a small dot in the land and label the city "Enoch". Cain named this city after his firstborn son. We don't know the exact location, only that it was east of Eden. (Genesis 4:16-17)

 ## "Harvest Fun": Games & Activities

- "Mom Says" - This game is to be played like Simon Says. Mom will give a command such as touch your toes, do five jumping jacks, walk like a duck, etc. Everyone must do exactly as she says...if she begins the command with, "Mom says". If she doesn't say this first and someone starts to perform the command, they're out. Stress how important it is to listen and obey. Cain did not carefully listen to and obey God's commands.

- Bounce Back with Kindness - Take a ping pong ball and draw a smiley face on it. Make up different scenarios and write them down on index cards or use "Kid's Choices" pocket card game from a Christian bookstore. (This card set has dilemmas for ages 6-11 that must be solved using Biblical principles. The cards cost around $6.00.) Some examples might include: You got a new bike for Christmas. Your friend wants to ride on it. You let him/her ride it and they accidentally run over a nail in the street and flatten the tire. Or, while standing in line at the movies, someone cuts in front of you. When you're ready to play, read a scenario out loud then let the child bounce the ball off the floor or wall and catch it. As he holds it, let him respond as to how he could "bounce back" with kindness to the situation when tempted to be angry. Cain did not handle his anger in the proper way and it led to a disastrous result.

"Digging Deeper": Research

- Names had great importance in the Bible. We're told the meaning of Cain's name ("gotten or acquired" - Eve said she had gotten him from the Lord), but what does Abel's name mean?

- We see that many of Cain's descendants were talented, skilled men. Research metalworking in bronze and iron. Research animal husbandry (raising livestock). Research how to make ancient musical instruments like harps and flutes. Remember that God created man in His own image. From the very beginning of time, man had intelligence and skill to do many amazing things.

"Food for Thought": Puzzles

- Who Am I? or What Am I? - Three clues will be given for each person or thing. Try to guess it using the clues given. You might want to give bonus points for guessing it right on clue one or clue two. Put your thinking caps on! Answers are provided in the Answer Key.

1. Clue #1) I am a small part of a large group. Clue #2) I have to follow my leader. Clue #3) I was offered by Abel. _____

2. Clue #1) I am a shepherd. Clue #2) I have a brother. Clue #3) I am the second born of Adam and Eve. _____

3. Clue #1) Every one has some of me. Clue #2) Without me there's no life. Clue #3) I cried out to God from the ground. _____

4. Clue #1) I am a father. Clue #2) I am a farmer. Clue #3) My son was killed. _____

5. Clue #1) I was created on the third day. Clue #2) I can be stubborn to some people. Clue #3) Crops grow in me. _____

6. Clue #1) I am a farmer. Clue #2) I have a brother. Clue #3) God placed a mark on me. _____

7. Clue #1) I am something God commanded. Clue #2) I was brought to the Lord by

different people. Clue #3) One of me was accepted by God and one was rejected.

_____

8. Clue #1) I was created on the sixth day. Clue #2) Adam gave me my name. Clue #3) I am the mother of Cain and Abel. _____

9. Clue #1) I am not liked by God. Clue #2) If you do not rule over me, I lie at your door. Clue #3) I am a separator. _____

10. Clue #1) I am always on the run. Clue #2) I am often hunted. Clue #3) Cain was one. _____

- Crossword – The following page contains a crossword puzzle using clues from this lesson. Answers are provided in the Answer Key.

Genesis 4

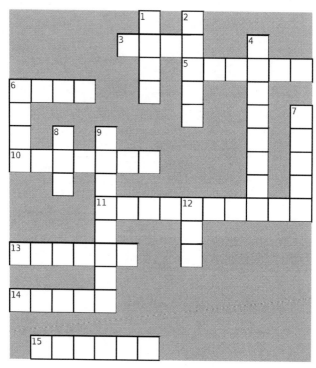

Across

3 Who was Adam and Eve's firstborn?

5 This would no longer yield its strength to Cain

6 Cain _____ to God

10 "Where is your _____?"

11 Cain said his was too great

13 What occupation did Cain have?

14 This cried to God from the ground

15 Cain _____ his brother Abel

Down

1 This was placed on Cain

2 How did Cain feel when God rejected his offering?

4 Cain was a _____ and vagabond

6 Abel offered this

7 Cain offered this

8 Land Cain went to

9 What occupation did Abel have?

12 God warned Cain that this was lying at his door

"Fruits Of Our Labor": Crafts

- Make models to represent Cain and Abel's sacrifices - Cain offered the fruit of the ground. Use play-doh or modeling clay to make some fruits and vegetables and maybe a platter or basket to put them in. Use an empty toilet paper roll to make a sheep. Cover the roll with glue and glue on cotton balls. Use two short pipe cleaners (black or brown) to make legs. Form them in a V-shape, invert and insert into the tube for legs and feet. (Before inserting "legs", poke a hole in the tube with scissors tips.) Draw a sheep's face (or trace the sheep's face on the creation card in Appendix B), cut it out and glue it on one end of the cotton-covered tube.

- Build an altar - Use Legos or building blocks to make altars for Cain and Abel's sacrifices. (The sheep might need a bigger altar!)

Lesson 4: Noah and the Ark

Text: Genesis 6 – 7:10

"Growing In The Word": Lesson Text & Discussion

Read Genesis 6:1-3. At the end of our last lesson, we studied about the ungodly descendants of Cain. Remember Lamech, the first polygamist and another murderer? Cain's family chose to turn away from following God, but Seth was a godly man like his brother Abel had been. Seth's family followed God faithfully. However, we see that a disturbing problem arose as the earth grew more populated with people: the ungodly started intermarrying with the godly. Why do you think this was a problem? (Answers may vary.) Do you think it is wise for someone who is trying to follow God faithfully to marry someone who has chosen to turn away from God? **Read II Corinthians 6:14-15.** The phrase "unequally yoked" is referring to an illustration of a team of oxen. A wooden bar called a "yoke" would join two oxen together to pull a plow or a cart, etc. If one oxen was much taller than the other or one was much stronger than the other, they would not pull together equally and whatever task they were trying to complete would be extremely difficult or would fail. It is never a good idea for a follower of God to join himself with one who is not or they will be like the unequally yoked oxen – always struggling to work together and not succeeding. Because of these marriages, the world gradually fell further and further into sin and farther and farther away from God. The Lord gives a time frame for how long the people have to repent before the destruction of the world comes by the flood. How long does God say it will be? (120 years) During this time, Noah is not only building the ark, but preaching to the people, trying to turn them from their wickedness back to God. **II Peter 2:5** refers to Noah as a "preacher of righteousness". We need to remember that God is always merciful. He gave the people 120 years of warning through the preaching of Noah and seeing the ark being built before their very eyes. They were given the choice to obey God and be saved or to continue being wicked and face the flood.

Read Genesis 6:4. There were real giants on the earth both at this time and after the flood. Goliath wasn't the only one!

Read Genesis 6:5-7. How bad was the wickedness of the people at this time? It is hard to imagine, but the Bible says that *every* thought they had was evil. The Lord was grieved at the sinful and violent state of the earth. What did He say He was going to destroy? (Man, animals, and birds) What about the promise He made in Genesis 3:15? How can a Savior come to save the world if everyone would be destroyed? Well, not every person was evil. In fact, there was a man who was still very faithful to God.

Read Genesis 6:8. Noah found grace or favor with God. He was a righteous man even though almost everyone else around him was wicked. He serves as a good example to us. Sometimes it's hard to obey God and do what's right especially if we feel like no one else around us is, but following God is *always* the right thing to do and He will help us do it.

Read Genesis 6:9-10. How is Noah described in these verses? (Just, faithful, upright, righteous, one who walked with God) Who were his three sons? (Shem, Ham and Japheth)

Read Genesis 6:11-13. What was the earth filled with? (Violence and corruption)

Read Genesis 6:14-16. God gave Noah **specific** instructions on how to build the ark and Noah followed every one of them completely. We also need to make sure we obey **everything**

God commands and not just pick and choose the parts we want to obey. What kind of wood was Noah to use? (Gopherwood) *Bonus: Here's an easy way to remember that – Question: What did Noah tell his three sons to do? Answer: Go-for-wood! What was the ark to be covered with inside and out? (Pitch) This was to waterproof the ark. The pitch would have been a thick tar-like substance probably derived from resin from trees. Many rooms and compartments were made in the ark for the animals and for food storage. The ark had three levels or stories. There was as much room inside the ark as 522 railroad cars and it was longer than a football field! The measurements of the ark were 300 cubits long, 50 cubits wide and 30 cubits high. So, what's a cubit? It was a unit of measurement generally measured by the length of a man's forearm from his elbow to the tip of his middle finger. On average this would be 18 inches. How many windows and doors were there? (One each)

Read Genesis 6:17-18. Do you know what a covenant is? It is an agreement between two parties. God makes a covenant with Noah to save him and his family. How many people total were going to be saved in the ark? (8) Who were they? (Noah, his wife, Noah's three sons and their wives)

Read Genesis 6:19-21. How many of each living creature was Noah to bring in the ark? (Two of each, male and female) For what purpose? (To keep them alive) God is preserving mankind and a remnant of the animals to replenish the earth after the flood. What else is Noah told to gather? (Food for their provisions)

Read Genesis 6:22. How much of what God said did Noah obey? (He obeyed ALL that God commanded.) He didn't just do the things that made sense to him or that were easy. He carried out every command God gave him down to the last detail. Would to God that we follow Noah's example of total obedience to ALL of God's commands!

Read Genesis 7:1-3. Noah is described as living righteously before God. To be righteous means "to do that which is right." Do you think that would have been easy for Noah and his family at a time when all of the world around them was so wicked? More detailed instructions are given concerning the animals. There are to be two of each unclean, male and female, and seven of the clean animals, male and female. How many of each kind of bird was to be taken on the ark? (7 of each bird, male and female)

Read Genesis 7:4. After Noah, his family, and the animals were on the ark, how many days was it before the flood began? (7) God had them safely secured and settled in the ark before any of the destruction started.

Read Genesis 7:5. Again we're told that Noah did ALL that God commanded. This is so important. Noah didn't just do part of what God said or the things he thought made sense. No, he trusted God and completely obeyed. This is why Noah found grace in the eyes of the Lord; God knew the faithful, obedient heart Noah had.

Read Genesis 7:6. How old was Noah when the flood came? (600) Can you imagine being six hundred years old? Much less, working on a massive building project at that age?

Read Genesis 7:7-10. The flood is now going to begin. Our next lesson will cover the time of the flood in Genesis chapters 7-9.

*Some good resources to enhance your study of Noah's ark: *The True Story of Noah's Ark* by Tom Dooley; *Noah's Ark: Thinking Outside the Box* DVD by Answers in Genesis.

<u>Review Questions</u>:   (Answers are provided in the Answer Key.)

1. How many years warning did God give mankind before He sent the flood?

2. Noah is called a preacher of what?

3. How bad was man's wickedness?

4. What did God say He would destroy?

5. Noah found _____ in the eyes of the Lord.

6. How does the Bible describe Noah?

7. Who were Noah's sons?

8. What was the earth filled with?

9. What was the ark made of?

10. What was it covered with inside and out?

11. What were the dimensions (measurements) of the ark?

12. How many windows and doors were there?

13. How many decks or stories were there?

14. Whom did God establish His covenant with?

15. How many people were saved in the ark?

16. How many of each kind of animal were taken into the ark?

17. What else was Noah to take into the ark?

18. How many days after Noah and his family and the animals went into the ark did the flood come?

19. How old was Noah when the flood began?

20. How much of God's commands did Noah obey?

 "Putting Down Roots": Memory Work

• Memorize Genesis 6:8

• Memorize Genesis 6:22

• Memorize the measurements of the ark – 300x50x30 cubits

"Farther Afield": Map Work

• There are no mapping activities for this lesson.

 "Harvest Fun": Games & Activities

• "Place the Animals in the Ark" - On a large piece of poster board, draw an ark with the gangplank lowered in the middle. Cut out pictures of animals from magazines or coloring books. You may want to use some of the pairs of animals from the first lesson's game. You may want to laminate the pictures or cover them with contact paper in order to reuse them. Place double stick tape on the back of each picture. Place the ark picture on the wall. Blindfold each player and let them try to place the animals on the gangplank going into the ark. Use the game to review and discuss how many of each kind of animal God told Noah to put in the ark.

✻ • "Build an Ark through Obedience" - Gather enough Legos or building blocks for each player to build an ark and distribute evenly among them. Read an obedience situation to a player. If he answers correctly, he has ten seconds to work on his ark. When time is up, the next player gets a chance to answer the next situation correctly and ten seconds to work on his ark and so on. Whoever completes their ark first, wins.

*Remember Genesis 6:22. To obey is to do <u>all</u> and with the right attitude. Listen to the situation and answer yes or no.

1. Mom asks you to take out the trash. You're in the middle of your favorite TV show. You wait until it's over and then do it. Did you completely obey? (No, not if she wanted it done immediately. What if Noah had built the ark like God said, but waited a year to get started? Would that have been obeying ALL that God commanded?)

2. Your teacher gives you a page of math problems. You do them all except one that you can't figure out. When asked if you're finished, you answer, "yes" because you really want to go out and play and you did do most of them. Did you obey? (No, you must answer truthfully.)

3. Mom comes home from the store and asks for help carrying the groceries. You're in the middle of an exciting book – it's at the best part! But you cheerfully put it

down, jump up, and run out to help. Did you obey? (Yes)

4. Your dad wants you to do some yard work on Saturday and says he needs your help. You had wanted to sleep in and then invite a friend over, but you tell him, "Sure, Dad, I'll be glad to help." Did you obey? (Yes, if you mean what you say.)

5. An adult at your church tells you to pick up some candy wrappers out of the pews and then leaves the auditorium. Your friends are waiting for you outside, so you grab a few, throw them away, then head out. Did you obey? (No, not if you didn't finish the task completely.)

6. Mom asks you to clean your room. You say, "Okay", but when she leaves the room, you start slamming toys in the toy box and kicking the laundry down to the hamper in anger. Did you obey? (No. Yes, you cleaned your room, but it is not total obedience when done with a bad attitude. True obedience comes from the heart and is done willingly and cheerfully.)

7. Your grandmother just got out of the hospital and needs some housecleaning chores done. She'd like your help. You tell her you'd be happy to do it and start gathering cleaning supplies to take to her house. You even think about what else she might need help with besides chores and plan to do those things also. Did you obey? (Yes)

8. You get into trouble and are told to sit in a chair until you're told to get up. You sit down with arms crossed and a sour look. You say, "I'm sitting down, but on the inside I'm standing up." Did you obey? (No. You are sitting as you were told, but your attitude is not one of obedience.)

9. Your dad tells the family that he'll take everyone out for ice cream as soon as their rooms are clean. Everyone else is done quick, but your room is a mess and will take much longer to clean so you shove everything under your bed. Your dad comes in to inspect, sees a clean floor and room and says, "Good job! Let's go!" You smile and skip out to the car. Did you obey? (No)

10. You're at the library. A librarian walks up to you and asks you to please pick up the paper on the floor by your foot and throw it away. It's not your trash, but you smile and do it anyway. Did you obey? (Yes)

Some of these situations are tough and some of the answers are tough as well, but we need to remember what total obedience is. In our family, we say: "Obey right away, all the way, in a cheerful way." Sometimes we only do part of this formula and think that is good enough, but it isn't. If we have trouble obeying our parents, teachers, or other adults and people in authority over us, then we will have trouble obeying God. Let's all practice (like Noah) obeying ALL the way, cheerfully and diligently.

"Digging Deeper": Research

- Read Genesis chapter 5. On a piece of paper, start with Adam and write the name of each descendant in order down the page ending with Noah. (There should be ten names.) Look up the meaning of each name and write it down next to the name. Now read the name meanings in order. Depending on the name meanings you look up, you will read something very interesting! (Answers appear in the Answer Key.)

- Which man from the list above died the year the flood came and how old was he when he died? Hint: He was the oldest man that ever lived.

- The measurements of the ark are given in cubits. A cubit was a measurement from the tip of a man's middle finger to his elbow, approximately 18 inches. Convert the measurements of the ark from cubits to feet.

 # "Food For Thought": Puzzles

Answers to both puzzles appear in the Answer Key.

- Animal Matching Puzzle #1 – Match the name of the animal to what it is.

bull	female donkey
sow	male deer
jenny	male duck
drake	female horse
doe	female pig
tom	male alligator
jill	female fox
gander	female goat
buck	male chicken
vixen	female deer
rooster	male turkey
nanny	female kangaroo
mare	male goose

• Animal Matching Puzzle #2 – Match the baby animal to its name.

colt	baby skunk
joey	baby frog
calf	baby pig
tadpole	baby swan
cygnet	baby horse
pup	baby bird
hatchling	baby whale
kit	baby panda
fawn	baby kangaroo
shoat	baby goat
cub	baby shark
kid	baby deer
gosling	baby alligator
chick	baby goose

 "Fruits Of Our Labor": Crafts

• Construct a model of the ark – Most of the "cutesy" pictures we see of Noah's ark are nowhere near what it really looked like! Try building a model that is more in line with how the Bible describes it. Take two 1 quart containers (like ½ and ½ or milk cartons). Cut off the tops of each so you have two rectangular shapes. Put the two cut ends together and secure with strong tape to give you one long box. Paint it brown or cover with brown construction paper. You may want to draw or paint black lines along it to look like "planks" of wood. Draw, paint, or cut a door in the side. Cut a 4 inch x 12 inch strip of brown construction paper. Score and fold down a 1 inch edge on each of the two long sides leaving a flat 2 inch wide strip on top. Score and fold down a 1 inch edge on each short end. Cut the two short scored lines on each end so you can fold in the short tabs and tape it from behind. When complete you should have an enclosed "roof" to set down on top of the ark. Secure with tape or glue. *You may want to save your ark model for the next lesson.

• Ark mural – Take a large piece of poster board or butcher paper. Draw an ark and any landscape you'd like. Draw animals going to the ark or use animal stickers.

Lesson 5: The Flood

Text: Genesis 7:11-9:17

"Growing In The Word": Lesson Text & Discussion

(For dramatic effect in this lesson, play a nature CD of a rainstorm in the background.)

Read Genesis 7:11-12. The month and day of the beginning of the flood are given here which will help us figure out later how long it lasted. There were *two* sources of water during the flood. The "windows of heaven" opened, which would be the rain, and the "fountains of the deep" opened up. What were those? When the flood occurred, the majority of the water didn't come from above, but from beneath. There were volcanic eruptions in the oceans and great movement of the tectonic plates of the earth's crust. Water literally broke through and burst forth from worldwide underground eruptions. Someone once described it as picturing the earth as one huge ball of aluminum foil that God took in His hand and squeezed. Combine that with torrential worldwide storms for forty days and forty nights and you can see what a picture of worldwide destruction by water looks like!

Read Genesis 7:13-16. There are 8 souls safe in the ark because they were in total obedience to God and His word. Who shut the door of the ark? (God) Only 8 people in the whole world will survive this flood. Could there have been more? Yes! The ark was a means of salvation. One had to believe in God's Word that was preached through Noah, repent and turn to God, and then go into the ark where God provided a way to be saved from the coming destruction, but only 8 people chose to do that. **Read I Peter 3:20-21.** Noah's ark was a means of salvation through water, and it also served as a type or shadow of how we receive salvation. What does verse 21 say saves us? (Baptism)

Read Genesis 7:17-20. As the flood waters rise, the ark floats safely on top of the water. Why do you think the Bible mentions how high the water rose above the highest mountain? It has to do with the draft of a boat. The draft is how much of the boat sinks down in the water. The specifications of the ark were such that even as it sat in the water, God had enough water covering the mountain tops so that the ark could sail safely over top of them without ripping the bottom of the ark. Do you think that God thought of everything? Absolutely!

Read Genesis 7:21-24. There is no doubt from these verses that the flood was worldwide and not local. There was complete destruction. How long did the waters prevail (stay) on the earth after the 40 days of rain were over? (150 days) So Noah and his family were in the ark for 7 days before the flood began, then there were 40 days of rain, then the waters stayed on the earth for 150 days after that. So far they've spent a total of 197 days in the ark which is about six and a half months.

Read Genesis 8:1. Did God forget about Noah? No! When the Bible says, "God remembered..." it means He is about to take action regarding someone or something. He is now going to start letting the waters recede and preparing the earth to once again be fit for man and animals to live on it. Have you ever gone outside after several days of heavy rain? You will usually see big puddles of standing water that may take several days to dry up and then there's usually a muddy mess left behind until the sun dries it all up. Now picture the earth as the flood waters start to go down. First you would start seeing mountain tops appear and eventually tree tops and so on until there's just big puddles on the ground. Then you'd have soggy, muddy ground that would take quite a while to dry up and firm up so it could be walked on. Then new grass and plants need to grow so that the animals will have food to eat when they come out of the ark. Noah and the animals will have to continue to live in the ark for quite a while longer even though the flood itself is over.

Read Genesis 8:2-4. When and where did the ark rest? (On the 17th day of the 7th month in the mountains of Ararat.) Some people say the ark rested on Mt. Ararat, but it is not one mountain but a mountain range called Ararat. It is located in the modern day country of Turkey.

Read Genesis 8:5. After the ark landed, it was still three months later before the tops of the mountains were seen.

Read Genesis 8:6-9. What two kinds of birds did Noah send out of the ark? (A raven and a dove) Why did Noah send out the birds? (He's trying to see how much of the water has dried up.) Are there dry trees anywhere that the birds may live in? (Not yet) The raven kept flying around looking for a spot and the dove returned back to the ark.

Read Genesis 8:10-11. How long did Noah wait before sending the dove out again? (7 days) What does the dove bring back this time? (An olive leaf) Ah! Greenery is now being seen by the dove.

Read Genesis 8:12. How long does Noah wait before sending out the dove for the third time? (7 more days) Why doesn't the dove come back? (It had found a home and stayed there.)

Read Genesis 8:13-14. It has now been a full year that they've been in the ark. The earth is dry, but Noah still waits. Why? He's waiting for God's permission to leave the ark and instructions on what to do next.

Read Genesis 8:15-19. The time has finally come! Now God instructs them to leave the ark. The earth is ready to sustain life once again. The total amount of time they have spent in the ark is 1 year and 10 days. (Genesis 7:11 tells us the flood began in the 600th year of Noah's life on the 17th day of the 2nd month and 8:14-16 says Noah was told to leave the ark on the 27th day of the 2nd month which would have been in the 601st year of Noah's life. Total = 1 year, 10 days)

Read Genesis 8:20-22. What is the first thing Noah does? (He builds an altar and sacrifices to God.) This is an act of worship. Noah is thankful for God's mercy and deliverance. God is pleased with the sacrifice and promises never to destroy the earth by a worldwide flood again.

Read Genesis 9:1-4. God's first command to them now is to have children! Fill the earth again with people. They are also now permitted to hunt animals for food. Remember that in the beginning, only vegetation was permitted for them to eat. They can now eat meat, but not the blood of the animal because life is in the blood.

Read Genesis 9:5-7. God institutes capital punishment. That is, if you take a life, then you pay with your own life. Why? (Man is created in the image of God; he's special.) God considers life to be very precious.

Read Genesis 9:8-17. God makes a covenant with Noah and all people. He will never again destroy the earth with water. What do you think Noah or someone else might think the next time they hear a thunderstorm start? Would they be afraid that God wasn't going to keep His promise? God gave Noah a sign to show that He would always keep His promise. What was the sign? (A rainbow) To this day, we still see rainbows in the sky. God is still reminding us thousands of years later that He is keeping His promise and we need not be afraid.

<u>Review Questions</u>:   (Answers are provided in the Answer Key.)

1. How old was Noah when the flood began?

2. How long did it rain?

3. What were the two sources of water?

4. Who shut the door of the ark?

5. How many days did the waters prevail on the earth?

6. When and where did the ark rest?

7. What two kinds of birds did Noah send out?

8. Which one returned?

9. Why did Noah wait to leave the ark?

10. When did they leave the ark?

11. How long were they in the ark altogether?

12. When they came out, was the ground soggy and muddy or completely dry?

13. What was the first thing Noah did?

14. What did God now give permission for man to eat?

15. What was man not allowed to eat and why?

16. God now institutes capital punishment or the death penalty for killing someone. What is the reason given?

17. What is a covenant?

18. God made a covenant with whom?

19. What did God promise?

20. What was the sign of the covenant?

 "Putting Down Roots": Memory Work

- Memorize Genesis 9:6

- Memorize Genesis 9:13

"Farther Afield": Map Work

Map 5

- Locate the mountains of Ararat. What modern day country are they in?

 ### "Harvest Fun": Games & Activities

- Ark Races – Build two model arks from the Crafts section of the last lesson. Have an ark race in the bathtub or a swimming pool. Blow like the wind behind your ark and try to cross the finish line of safety first.

- Rainbows – How do we see rainbows? What makes the colors? Try making a rainbow. Take a clear glass and fill it 2/3 full of water. Hold it up above a plain white sheet of paper near a window where the sun is shining. Watch the sunlight pass through the water, refract (bend), and form a rainbow on your sheet of paper.

 ### "Digging Deeper": Research

- Clean/Unclean Animals – God told Noah to take 7 pairs of clean animals and one pair of unclean animals into the ark. What were clean and unclean animals? (Leviticus 11; Deuteronomy 14:1-21)

- Flood Stories – Many ancient cultures had some type of flood story. See how many different ones you can find. What countries did they come from? What are the similarities with the Biblical account? What are the differences?

 ### "Food For Thought": Puzzles

- Word Scramble – Unscramble the letters to make words from this lesson. Answers are provided in the Answer Key.

niar	_____	tyfor	_____
lmiansa	_____	dniw	_____
ntfoauins	_____	verna	_____
eovd	_____	ciifecasr	_____
obnariw	_____	enctovan	_____

- Numbers Matching – Draw a line from the number to what it matches. Answers are provided in the Answer Key.

600	number of days water stood on the earth
7	number of Noah's sons
2	length of ark in cubits
40	age of Noah at the beginning of the flood
150	days and nights of rain
7	number of people saved on the ark
3	number of pairs of unclean animals
8	number of cubits the waters prevailed above the mountains
300	number of days Noah waited before sending out the dove
15	number of clean animals
17	day of the month the ark rested on the mountains of Ararat

"Fruits Of Our Labor": Crafts

- "Making Waves" bottle – Use a 2 liter bottle or small glass jars (like baby food), water, blue food coloring, and mineral oil or baby oil. Fill bottle or jar 1/3 full of water. Tint with blue coloring to make a light blue color. Continue to fill the bottle or jar another 1/3 with mineral or baby oil. For extra sparkle, you can add white or silver glitter. Hot glue or superglue lid on. Turn bottle or jar on its side and tilt back and forth to make waves.

- Rainbow bookmark – Cut white card stock 2 inches wide by 6 inches long. On the top half of the bookmark, color a rainbow. On the bottom half, copy Genesis 9:13. Laminate your bookmark or cover it with contact paper.

- Rainmaker – You will need an empty paper towel tube, wax paper, rubber bands, and dry rice. Before you start, you may want to decorate your cardboard tube with crayons, markers, or paint. Then cut two circles out of wax paper larger than the openings of the tube. Place one large circle of wax paper over one end of the tube and secure it tightly with a rubber band. Place rice inside the tube. Fewer grains will make a quieter sound. Place the second circle of wax paper over the other end of the tube and secure with a rubber band. Trim your circles if needed. Now shake your rainmaker and listen to the rain!

Lesson 6: The Tower of Babel

Text: Genesis 11:1-9

"Growing In The Word": Lesson Text & Discussion

Read Genesis 11:1-2. For many years after the flood, people spoke just one common language and lived together in one central location. What location did they live in? (The land of Shinar) What modern day country do you think this might be? Hint: It is also where the garden of Eden was generally thought to be located. (Iraq) Was it okay for all of the people to live in just one location or did God have something else in mind? Keep reading to find out.

Read Genesis 11:3-4. What did the people decide to build and for what reason? Why would this bring God's displeasure? The people want to build a great tower that will reach the heavens (an early skyscraper!). They are building a city around it as well. They are baking their own bricks and making asphalt for mortar. Again we see clearly that early people had great intelligence and skills to do many things – even to constructing a great tower with handmade materials! However, they are already demonstrating willful, prideful hearts as they state that they *don't* want to be scattered abroad on the earth, but prefer to live together in one location. After the flood, God had *wanted* the people to multiply and fill the earth once again. His desire was for them to be scattered all over the earth. They show their proud hearts when they boastfully say that the reason they want the tower built is to make a name for themselves. (Look at what *we* can do!)

Read Genesis 11:5-7. God is always aware of what people are doing and He sees the direction they're going. These people are united in their thinking and in their plans. What will they do next? Anything they want! Verse 6 says, *"nothing that they propose to do will be withheld from them"*. Notice in verse 7 we see *"let Us"*. This is again referring to the Trinity or Godhead (Father, Son, and Holy Spirit) just as in Genesis 1:26. The purpose of God giving them different languages was to force them to do the very thing they were refusing to do – disperse and spread out. It also prevented them from being a unified people who could make plans together. They were now forced to spread out into different parts of the world by groups of those who spoke the same language.

Read Genesis 11:8-9. The name of the place was called "Babel" because God confused their language. It is where we get our word "babble" which means to talk in a way that can't be understood. The building of the tower and subsequent city around it stopped as the people now scattered to different parts of the world. Notice the Bible says the Lord scattered them – as He had wanted them to do in the first place.

<u>Review Questions</u>:   (Answers are provided in the Answer Key.)

1. At the beginning of this lesson, how many languages were there?

2. Where did the people settle?

3. What building materials did they use?

4. What did they want to build?

5. For what reason?

6. Who came down to see the work?

7. What did God propose to do to stop the work?

8. Once He did this and they couldn't understand each other, what did God do?

9. What is the name given to that place?

10. Why is it called that?

 "Putting Down Roots": Memory Work

- Memorize the books of the Law in the Old Testament – Genesis, Exodus, Leviticus, Numbers, Deuteronomy

- Memorize the divisions of the Old Testament – Law, History, Poetry, Prophecy

  Law: Genesis-Deuteronomy

  History: Joshua-Esther

  Poetry: Job-Song of Solomon

  Prophecy: Isaiah-Malachi

 "Farther Afield": Map Work

Map 1

- Locate the land of Shinar – What ancient country would this be and what modern day country is it? Label them as well.

 "Harvest Fun": Games & Activities

- Tower to the Skies – Gather as many building blocks as possible for 2 people. On "Go", start stacking blocks to build a tower as high as you can before it comes crashing down. You have 15 seconds to build. Whoever's tower is the highest or is still standing when time is up is the winner.

• Coded Message – Make up your own special language or use a language that someone else doesn't understand. For example, maybe you know Spanish or Latin, but your friend does not. Then make a coded message for your friend or family member to figure out. Give them clues or a key to help them decipher your message. The trick is to get them to understand a language they're not familiar with at all.

"Digging Deeper": Research

• Brick-making – How did people in the Bible make their own bricks? Read about and write down the process or explain it to someone.

• World Languages – When God confused the language of the people, He scattered them to live in groups according to what language they spoke. Look at a world map. See how many different languages you can identify by country. For instance, the United States' primary language is English. What do they speak in Egypt, Denmark, India, Wales, etc.? Learning the history of languages can be interesting as well. When God confused the language of the people in Genesis 11, there weren't French and Spanish-speaking people. French and Spanish are two of five languages that came from one ancient language: Latin. What were the other three languages that came from Latin?

 ## "Food For Thought": Puzzles

• Coded Message –

___ ___ ___   ___ ___ ___ ___   ___ ___   ___ ___ ___ ___ ___
18 7 8   13 26 14 22   18 8   25 26 25 22 15

___ ___ ___ ___ ___ ___ ___   ___ ___ ___   ___ ___ ___ ___
25 22 24 26 6 8 22   7 19 22   15 12 9 23

__ __ __ __ __ __ __ __   __ __ __ __ __
24 12 13 21   6   8 22 23   7 19 22 18   9

__ __ __ __ __ __ __ __ .
15 26 13 20   6 26 20 22

Key to the Code:

F	N	R	U	A	G	O	S	V	C	H	T	D	I	E	B	W	K	Y	P	M	L
21	13	9	6	26	20	12	8	5	24	19	7	23	18	22	25	4	16	2	11	14	15

- Word Search – Tower of Babel (Answers are provided in the Answer Key.)

```
N P Y D R O L C A O E I O T E
B R I C K S C A T T E R E D R
E A A Y T O P D N E V A E H S
T N T T N L U E L G T R R C N
T I A F R H N P E I U G R T G
C H U M B O O S B C U A S S H
E S E A E E M V A U H B G A E
E D H K P E A O B N T O W E R
```

language	one	Shinar
bricks	tower	city
scattered	confuse	Babel
east	speech	mortar
build	heaven	Lord
people	earth	name

"Fruits Of Our Labor": Crafts

- Build a Tower – Design and build a tower out of big marshmallows or sugar cubes. Use peanut butter or frosting as "mortar".

- Shortbread Bricks – Here is a neat recipe to try. These will be fun to make and the best part is – they're edible!

Ingredients:

1 pound unsalted butter, room temperature, plus more for pans

4 cups all-purpose flour   1 cup sugar

1 ½ teaspoons salt   2 teaspoons vanilla extract

*For cinnamon bricks, add one tablespoon ground cinnamon to the flour mixture.

Preheat oven to 275 degrees. Butter five loaf pans (5 ¾ by 3 ¼) and set aside. In a mixing bowl, sift flour and salt. In a separate bowl, place the butter and beat with an electric mixer until light and fluffy, about 3 to 5 minutes. Add the sugar and continue beating until the mixture is very light in color and fluffy. Add the vanilla and blend. Add the reserved flour mixture, and combine on low speed, scraping sides with spatula, if necessary. Mix just until the flour is incorporated and the dough sticks together when pressed with your fingers. Divide the dough evenly among the prepared pans, spreading it about 1 ¼ inches thick. Smooth the tops and decorate by using a skewer to poke holes to create a pattern. Bake until firm and just starting to turn color, about 2 hours. You may need to re-prick the design as soon as it comes out of the oven. Remove the bricks from the pan, transfer to a cooling rack, and let them cool to room temperature. Slice them to serve.

- Stepping Stone – When the people were building the Tower of Babel, they made their bricks by hand. Today, you'll create your own stepping stone to be put in a flower bed, garden, pathway, etc. You will need: concrete mix (from the hardware store), a form or mold to pour it in (you can make your own from things like a recycled pizza box, shoe box, plastic ice cream tub, etc.), or you can buy a kit that includes the concrete or plaster and molds from a craft or hobby store. You might like to decorate your stone with your handprints, footprints, initials or things like marbles, beads or mosaic tiles. Mix the concrete or plaster according to the package directions and pour into the mold. Let it sit for about an hour, then personalize and decorate as desired. Let it dry completely.

Lesson 7: Abraham

Text: Genesis 12:1-7; 16; 21:1-21

"Growing In The Word": Lesson Text & Discussion

Read Genesis 12:1. Abram (God later changes his name to Abraham) left his father's house, his family, and his country. He left behind everything he'd ever known to go to a new, unfamiliar land. Do you think that was hard for him to do? Abram did this by faith. He believed in what God said and acted in obedient faith, trusting in God's promise. **Read Hebrews 11:8.**

Read Genesis 12:2-3. God makes three promises to Abram and they are very important:

1. God will make a great nation of him.

2. God will give him the land of Canaan.

3. Through Abraham, all families of the earth would be blessed. (Galatians 3:16 says that Christ would come through the line of Abraham. He is the blessing to all people.)

Read Genesis 12:4-7. Abram takes his family and possessions and goes in obedient faith, trusting in the promises of God. One of the family members that goes with him is his nephew, Lot. How old is Abram when this journey begins? (75) God leads him to the land of Canaan, the land that is promised to the descendants of Abraham. He is grateful to God for His promises and providence. What does he build and why? (He builds an altar to worship the Lord.) If you study the life of Abraham, you will see that wherever he goes, he builds an altar in order to worship the Lord.

Read Genesis 16:1-2. Abram's wife, Sarai (her name will later be changed by God to Sarah), had never had children. She thought the Lord was preventing her from having any. She and Abram were both old in years and Sarai wondered how God was going to keep His promise to Abram that a great nation would come from him when he didn't even have any children. She decided to take matters into her own hand. BIG mistake! What she is about to do will cause trouble for **years** to come. Sometimes, it is hard for me to wait, maybe it is hard for you too, but trusting in God and having faith in Him means waiting on *His* timetable. Another problem we see here is that she told Abram what to do, and he obeyed her instead of trusting in God to keep His promise in His own time.

Read Genesis 16:3-4. Sarai thinks she has the answer to their problem and gives her Egyptian maid, Hagar, to Abram as another wife. Do you think going against God's plan is ever a good solution? (No!) Hagar gets pregnant and now starts to despise, or hate Sarai, her mistress. This will also cause problems as the two women will no longer get along well with each other. Abram's family had lived in Canaan for ten years, so how old would he be now? (85)

Read Genesis 16:5-6. Once Sarai sees that Hagar is pregnant and now has an arrogant attitude about it ("I'm having a baby and you're not!"), Sarai is angry, complains to Abram (and even blames him!), then deals harshly with Hagar. Hagar runs away. Now, whose fault is all of this? Whose bright idea was it to interfere with God's plan? (Sarai's!) Sometimes we think we know better than God and then act differently than He would have us act. We find out that when we try to take control, things don't work out so well. Remember Eve in the Garden of Eden? We need to learn to always trust in God.

Read Genesis 16:7-9. The Angel of the Lord finds Hagar in the wilderness and asks her what she's doing. She tells him she's running away. What does the Angel tell her to do? (Return to her mistress and submit to her) Even though Hagar hadn't been treated well, it was still not right for her to run away. She is told to go back and submit to Sarai as her maid. Did you notice that "the Angel of the Lord" has a capital "A"? Whenever you see this title in the Bible, this is talking about Jesus himself. It is called a "theophenes" or pre-incarnate Christ which simply means Jesus appeared as a man or an angel before he came to earth to be born in a manger. There are several instances in the Old Testament where Jesus appears as "The Angel of the Lord" and speaks to someone. Hagar is one of them.

Read Genesis 16:10-12. God doesn't neglect to look out for Hagar. The Angel of the Lord makes her a promise. She also will have many descendants through the son that is to be born, and then he also tells her some things about her child before he's even born. What would his name be? (Ishmael) What kind of man will he be? (Wild) Will he get along well with people? (No)

Read Genesis 16:13-14. Hagar names the place where she's spoken to the Angel. What does she call it? ("El Roi" which means "God Who Sees.")

Read Genesis 16:15-16. Hagar does as she's told and returns to give birth to her son, Ishmael. How old was Abram when Ishmael was born? (86) Can you imagine being a first time father at that age?

Read Genesis 21:1-3. God finally blesses Sarah with a son and he is the son of promise. Notice that verse 1 says the Lord did this **as He said** and **as He had spoken**. She would have had to wait 14 years from the time she thought about giving Hagar to Abraham, but God did exactly as He promised and gave she and Abraham a son. She never had to take matters into her own hand, did she? The child is named Isaac which means "laughter". Do you know why he was named that? It served as a reminder that both Abraham and Sarah had laughed when they were told they would have a son. **Read Genesis 17:15-17** and **18:10-12.**

Read Genesis 21:4-7. This is 14 years after Ishmael is born. How old is Abraham when Isaac is born? Remember, he was 86 when Ishmael was born. (100)

Read Genesis 21:8-11. A great feast was thrown for Isaac when he was still a very little boy. What is Ishmael doing? (He is mocking or making fun of Isaac.) Do you think maybe Ishmael is just a little jealous of his younger half brother? Sarah sees this all too clearly and wants Ishmael gone. Abraham is conflicted about this because after all, Ishmael is his son too.

Read Genesis 21:12-13. God tells Abraham not to worry, but to do as Sarah wishes. God will still make a great nation of Ishmael as He promised to do.

Read Genesis 21:14-16. Abraham sends Hagar and Ishmael away with provisions, but after a time they run out and they're all alone out in the wilderness. What does Hagar think will happen to them? (She thinks that they'll die.)

Read Genesis 21:17-19. An angel speaks to Hagar from heaven reassuring her that God will take care of them. What does she then see? (A well of water)

Read Genesis 21:20-21. Where does Ishmael grow up? (Wilderness of Paran) What does he become? (Archer) His mother gets him a wife from Egypt when he's grown. Why do you think she does this? (Remember, she's an Egyptian. Egypt is her homeland.)

Review Questions: (Answers are provided in the Answer Key.)

1. Who called Abraham to leave his home country?

2. What were the three promises God made to Abraham?

3. How old was Abraham when he left his home?

4. Who was Sarah's maid?

5. What country was she from?

6. What did Sarah do when she thought she couldn't have children?

7. Was this a good idea?   Why or why not?

8. Who was Hagar's son born to Abraham?

9. How old was Abraham when his first son was born?

10. Who was the "son of promise" born to Sarah and Abraham?

11. What does his name mean?

12. How old was Abraham when he was born?

13. Did the two brothers get along?

14. Where did Ishmael go to grow up?

15. What country was his wife from?

 ## "Putting Down Roots": Memory Work

- Memorize Genesis 12:3
- Memorize Hebrews 11:8

 ## "Farther Afield": Map Work

Map 2, Map 3

- Locate the city of Haran
- Locate the land of Canaan
- Locate the Wilderness of Paran
- Locate the country of Egypt

"Harvest Fun": Games & Activities

- Be a Sojourner – Abraham was a sojourner. A sojourner is someone who stays somewhere temporarily, or has no permanent home. Abraham traveled a while to get to Canaan then later, due to famine, traveled to Egypt. Then he went back to Canaan and moved around to different locations, never really having a permanent dwelling. At each location he resided, he built altars so he could always worship His heavenly Father. Now you can be a sojourner like Abraham. (You may even want to dress up in costume like Abraham.) Gather up supplies for a journey. What will you need? Clothing, food, cooking utensils/pots, a tent (sheet). What else might you need? Put your supplies together and wrap them in your "tent". Travel to a "distant country" (maybe your back yard or living room). Unpack and set up your tent. Make camp and remember to do the most important thing: build an altar and say a prayer to God.

- Isaac or Ishmael – Each player needs 2 index cards or pieces of paper. One should say "Isaac" and one "Ishmael". Let one person be the clue reader. As a clue is read, each player must decide the correct answer and hold up that name card. Be careful, there might be some trick questions! The player with the most right answers at the end of the game wins.

1. I am an expert with the bow. (Ishmael)

2. My name means "laughter". (Isaac)

3. My mother is Egyptian. (Ishmael)

4. My wife is Egyptian. (Ishmael)

5. My father was 100 years old when I was born. (Isaac)

6. I laughed at my younger brother. (Ishmael)

7. My parents threw a big feast for me. (Isaac)

8. My mother laughed when she was told I'd be born. (Isaac)

9. When my mother was pregnant with me, she ran away from home. (Ishmael)

10. An Angel of the Lord spoke to my mother. (Both!)

11. At one point in my life, I almost died in the wilderness. (Ishmael)

12. I am Abraham's child of promise. (Isaac)

13. God chose my name. (Both!)

14. My mother thought she'd never have children. (Isaac)

15. I grew up in the Wilderness of Paran. (Ishmael)

16. I grew up with my parents. (Isaac)

17. My mother was a maidservant. (Ishmael)

18. My mother was told I'd be a wild man. (Ishmael)

19. My brother was 14 years older than me. (Isaac)

20. Abraham is my father. (Both!)

- Planetarium show - Take a field trip to a planetarium and view the stars. God promised Abraham that he would have so many descendants they would look like the stars of the sky and be too numerous to count!

"Digging Deeper": Research

- Learn more about Abraham - Who was his half-sister? (Gen. 20:12) Was his wife Sarah a beautiful or plain woman? (Genesis 12:11) What did Abraham do when God told him Sarah would have a son? (Genesis 17:17) How many trained servants did Abraham have who were trained for war? (Genesis 14:14) Once during a famine in Canaan, Abraham had to travel to another land for food. Where did he go? (Genesis 12:10) God prophesied to Abraham that his descendants would be servants in a foreign land. How long did He say they'd be there? (Genesis 15:13)

- Ur of the Chaldeans - Abraham's family originally lived in the city of Ur of the Chaldeans in Mesopotamia. Ur was a very advanced civilization at that time. Research what life might have been like for Abraham's family when they lived in "the big city".

- "The Angel of the Lord" - We talked about this being Jesus in our lesson. Find other Old Testament examples where the "Angel of the Lord" appeared to and spoke with someone. Remember, the word "angel" must be capitalized to indicate it's the Lord. Notice if the people he spoke to called him "Lord" or worshiped him. Regular angels were not referred to as "Lord", nor are they permitted to be worshiped as they are not deity.

"Food For Thought": Puzzles

• Crossword Puzzle – Answers are provided in the Answer Key.

Across
2 Where Ishmael grew up
6 Abraham was one _____ when Isaac was born
7 Land promised to Abraham and his descendants
8 Abraham's nephew
9 In Abraham, all families of the earth would be _____
10 God promised Abraham to make of him a great _____
12 What "Isaac" means
14 Ishmael's wife was from here
16 The _____ of the Lord found Hagar

Down
1 Son of promise
3 Hagar's son
4 Abraham's age when Ishmael was born
5 Abraham's age when he left his home
11 Abraham built one wherever he went
13 Egyptian servant of Sarah
15 He changed Sarah's name

- Who Am I? - Use the three clues to guess the name of the person. Answers are in the Answer Key.

1. Clue #1) My uncle was rich. Clue #2) I went with him to Canaan. Clue #3) My wife turned into a pillar of salt. _____

2. Clue #1) I was a servant to a wealthy woman. Clue #2) I was Egyptian. Clue #3) I had a son named Ishmael. _____

3. Clue #1) God changed my name. Clue #2) I had a son when I was an old woman. Clue #3) My son's name means laughter. _____

4. Clue #1) My father was old when I was born. Clue #2) My mother took a wife for me from Egypt. Clue #3) My younger brother and I didn't get along. _____

5. Clue #1) God called me to leave my home. Clue #2) God promised all nations of the earth would be blessed through me. Clue #3) I laughed when God told me my wife was going to have a baby. _____

6. Clue #1) My birth was foretold to my parents. Clue #2) My parents waited a long time for me. Clue #3) My name means "laughter". _____

7. Clue #1) I found Hagar after she ran away. Clue #2) I gave her a message from the Lord. Clue #3) I told her to return home. _____

"Fruits Of Our Labor": Crafts

- Make a Name for Yourself - We read in the Bible that Isaac's name means "laughter". Find out what your name means and make a name plaque. Use a rectangular piece of thin wood, poster board, or card stock measuring about 5 inches wide by 10 inches long. If you're using wood, you may want to paint a background color first. Write or paint your name in large letters. Underneath it in smaller letters, write or paint the meaning of your name. Decorate your name plaque however you'd like and hang it in your room.

- Number the Stars - In Genesis 15:5, God promised Abraham that he would make of him a great nation with so many descendants they'd be like the stars in the sky (too many to count!). Using the star templates in Appendix B, trace as many stars as you'd like onto brightly colored or white poster board. For a cool effect, paint them with glow-in-the-dark paint and let them dry thoroughly before cutting out. Secure the stars all over your bedroom ceiling with double stick tape or craft putty. Watch for a beautiful effect when you turn your lights out at night and think of God's promise to Abraham.

Lesson 8: Abraham Offers Isaac

Text: Genesis 22:1-19

"Growing In The Word": Lesson Text & Discussion

Read Genesis 22:1-2. God did not desire a human sacrifice, but rather God was testing Abraham's faith to see whether Abraham would give up (sacrifice) what he loved most on earth for God. Can you imagine how Abraham must have felt as God commanded this of him? He had waited so many years for Isaac, the son of promise, to be born and now he loves this son so very dearly. Yet Abraham loves God more and has a tremendous faith in Him.

Read Genesis 22:3-4. Abraham doesn't question, cry, or complain. He begins to make preparations to go on the journey that is required to do what God has asked of him. Abraham and Isaac do not travel alone. How many servants go with them? (2) How many days do they have to travel to their destination, the land of Moriah? (3) Isaac does not yet know what is going to take place. He is probably enjoying the journey with his father and talking to him as they travel. Can you imagine what Abraham must be thinking and how he must be feeling?

Read Genesis 22:5. Abraham leaves his two servants and only takes Isaac with him to go worship God and to sacrifice to Him. Notice he tells the two servants, "**we** will come back to you". Abraham fully intends to offer Isaac as God asked and he is not lying when he says this, so what can he mean? **Hebrews 11:17-19** sheds some light on what Abraham believed would happen. He knew that Isaac was the "son of promise"; that is, he was the son through whom the great nation would come, so he cannot die without having children of his own. Abraham had full faith in the promises of God and knew that God does not lie so Abraham came to the only conclusion he could: God would raise Isaac from the dead and restore him back to Abraham. Abraham's faith is so strong and he truly believes this is what will take place which is why he tells the servants, "we will come back to you".

Read Genesis 22:6-8. Abraham takes what is needed for the sacrifice: fire, wood, a knife...but Isaac notices there's no lamb to offer. When he asks Abraham about the lamb, what does his father tell him? (God will provide the lamb.)

Read Genesis 22:9-12. Abraham prepares everything and then does what is probably the hardest thing he's ever had to do in his life: he binds his dear son, lays him on the altar and raises the knife in his hand. Who stops him? (The Angel of the Lord calls out from heaven and stops him.) God sees the great faith Abraham has as he has not withheld even his precious son, Isaac, from Him.

Read Genesis 22:13-14. Abraham sees a ram caught in a thicket and sacrifices him to the Lord. The ram takes the place of Isaac, sparing him. Abraham names the place, "Jehovah Jireh" which means "the Lord will provide". This is a very important passage for us to consider as we realize that this is a picture of what God did for us. We were the ones who were to be sacrificed, but Jesus took our place by dying on the cross. God provided a means for us to be saved. He provided the Lamb. (John 1:29) How thankful we are for that and how thankful Abraham must have been as well.

Read Genesis 22:15-18. God's promise to him from Genesis 12 is restated. He states again that Abraham's descendants will be countless like the stars of the sky. What else does he compare their numbers to? (The sand on the seashore) God is very pleased with Abraham's obedience and promises to bless him.

Read Genesis 22:19. Just as Abraham had said, both he and Isaac return to where the servants are waiting and they all return home to Beersheba.

Review Questions: (Answers are provided in the Answer Key.)

1. Who tested Abraham?

2. Where was Abraham to take Isaac and what was he to do with him?

3. How many days did they travel?

4. Who did Abraham say would come back?

5. What New Testament scripture tells us what Abraham thought would happen?

6. What question did Isaac ask his father?

7. What was Abraham's reply?

8. Who stopped Abraham?

9. What did God provide in place of Isaac?

10. What did Abraham call the place and what did it mean?

 "Putting Down Roots": Memory Work

- Memorize Genesis 22:8
- Memorize John 1:29

 "Farther Afield": Map Work

Map 2

- Locate the land of Moriah
- Locate the city of Beersheba

"Harvest Fun": Games & Activities

- "Listen to God" - Take sheets of paper and lay them on the floor in a way that outlines a path or maze. Blindfold a person and lead them to the beginning of the maze. Talk them through the maze in such a way that their feet never touch the pieces of paper. For example, you might say, "Take two steps forward. Now take one small step to the left. Now take three steps forward and stop. Now turn to the right...", etc. When you're finished, talk about how important it was that Abraham listened to God even when he couldn't see exactly what was going to happen. You can see pictures and instructions of this activity at the following link: http://pryorconvictions.com/blindfold-maze/

- Father Abraham – Have fun singing and acting out the "Father Abraham" song. Come up with some of your own motions for something different! If you're not familiar with the song, you can find the lyrics and motions on different sites on the internet. Just search "Father Abraham song".

"Digging Deeper": Research

- Names of God – Abraham calls the place of offering "The Lord will provide". What is that in Hebrew? (Jehovah Jireh) What are some other names of God and what do they mean? Make a list of the Hebrew titles of God in one column and the meanings of the names in another column.

- Land of Moriah – The exact location where Abraham took Isaac is not known. The Bible only indicates it as one of the mountains in the land of Moriah. However, this general area has a lot of Biblical history. Research this location to see what important cities, sites and events took place here or in the near vicinity.

 ## "Food For Thought": Puzzles

- Coded Message –

"——— ——— ———   ——— ——— ——— ———   ——— ——— ——— ——— ——— ——— ———
  20   12   23   4   18   15   15   11   9   12   5   18   23   22

——— ——— ———   ——— ——— ——— ———   ——— ——— ———   ———   ——— ——— ——— ——— ———
  7   19   22   15   26   14   25   21   12   9   26   25   6   9   13   7

——— ——— ——— ——— ——— ——— ——— ———."
  12   21   21   22   9   18   13   20

Key to the Code:

F	N	R	U	A	G	O	S	V	C	H	T	D	I	E	B	W	K	Y	P	M	L
21	13	9	6	26	20	12	8	5	24	19	7	23	18	22	25	4	16	2	11	14	15

*Who said this and to whom did he say it? _____

_____

- Word Search – A Word Search Puzzle for this lesson is on the following page. Answers are provided in the Answer Key.

```
E F I N K D L S A M N S N B R
D A I S I F O E M O A T R M O
I I H R A S E O G U S N G A R
V T E A E A R H W N R A E L F
O H F T H I C K E T A V O O I
R A T L A B R A H A M R A H T
P F O H T E C N E I D E B O O
R E I O F F E R I N G S K O D
```

Abraham	Isaac	Moriah	mountain
wood	offering	altar	angel
Lord	ram	thicket	knife
fire	lamb	obedience	faith
provide	servants		

 "Fruits Of Our Labor": Crafts

- Heart of Faith – Abraham demonstrated a heart of great faith in the Lord. Use red or pink play-doh or modeling clay to form a large heart. Use a different color or colors to make the letters F-A-I-T-H. Place the letters inside the heart and press gently. You may want to use a type of clay that will harden and set so that you can keep this and display it.

- Sacrifice scene – Draw or paint a picture of the scene where Abraham is about to offer Isaac. Don't forget to include the ram and the Angel of the Lord calling from heaven. You could do this in comic strip fashion and have three or four "frames" telling the story. This is actually a beautiful picture of the salvation we have in Christ as God provides His lamb to take our place just as the ram took the place of Isaac.

Lesson 9: Jacob & Esau

Text: Genesis 25:19-34; 27; 28:1-9

NN

"Growing In The Word": Lesson Text & Discussion

Read Genesis 25:19-28. Abraham's son, Isaac, married a woman named Rebekah. How old was Isaac when he married Rebekah? (40 years old) They had to wait many years for God to bless them with children. When He did, He blessed them with twins. How old was Isaac when they were born? (60) While Rebekah was still pregnant with them, they were already struggling within her. God told her before they were born that they were going to have trouble getting along! The younger would rule over the older. Esau was born first and his name means "hairy" because he was covered with hair when he was born. How does the Bible describe him when he was born? (Red and like a hairy garment!) Jacob was born second with his hand grabbing his brother's heel and his name means "supplanter" or "heel-grabber". Picture a ladder with someone standing on the top step. Then think of someone standing several rungs lower on the same ladder reaching up and grabbing the heel of the person at the top and pulling them down in order to get ahead of them. This will be what Jacob keeps doing with Esau – supplanting or taking his place in the family. Esau grew up to be an avid outdoorsman and a skillful hunter. What did Jacob like to do? (He liked to hang around the house, or tent in this case.)

Read Genesis 25:29-34. The birthright was very important; it had material benefits (the inheritance) but also involved the future spiritual leadership of the family. Esau cared so little for it that he sold it for a bowl of stew! This is why the Bible says he despised his birthright. Jacob is not without fault here either; he sees an opportunity to take advantage of his brother and get something for himself and he does it!

Read Genesis 27:1-4. Isaac is old and blind and thinks he is near death so he wants a "last special meal". His favorite thing to eat is the wild game that Esau hunts. What does he ask Esau to do for him? (Go hunting, then fix the food in his favorite way.)

Read Genesis 27:5-10. Mama Rebekah is listening and sees a way to get the blessing for her favored son, Jacob. She wants him to disguise himself as Esau and fool his father. Is it right for her to want to trick her husband? (No!)

Read Genesis 27:11-12. It's interesting that Jacob doesn't object to her plan, but rather doubts its success. He doesn't think he can effectually fool his father. Why does Jacob think the plan won't work? (Esau is a hairy man and Jacob is smooth-skinned.) Jacob knows as soon as his father touches him, he'll know who it really is and then there will be trouble! His mother won't take no for an answer. If there is any trouble, she is willing to take the blame for it.

Read Genesis 27:13-17. Rebekah has this all figured out. What food does she fix for her husband? (She prepares a young goat from the flock which is called a kid.) She uses some of the hairy skin of the goat to "disguise" Jacob by placing strips of it on the smooth part of his neck and on his hands. She even dresses Jacob in Esau's clothes so that he will smell like him. She then sends him in to his father with the dinner tray in his hands.

5/2/22

Read Genesis 27:18-20. Let the lies begin! As you keep reading, try to count how many lies Jacob tells his father. Notice in this passage Jacob even brings God into one of his lies by saying he was able to obtain the food so quickly because God brought it to him! How does God feel about lying? **Proverbs 6:16-17** says that one of the things the Lord hates is a lying tongue. God takes the sin of lying very seriously – and so should we.

Read Genesis 27:21-24. Isaac is confused. Why? (The voice is Jacob's, but the skin feels like Esau's.) People who are blind usually have other senses that are heightened. For instance, their sense of hearing or sense of smell will be much sharper than a seeing person's. Isaac keeps asking Jacob, "Are you *really* Esau?" He feels like Esau and smells like Esau, but he sounds like Jacob. Isaac just can't make sense of this.

Read Genesis 27:25-29. Isaac eats his meal and gives the blessing to Jacob. Notice all the good things Jacob will have or be according to the blessing. Most importantly, he will be the master or ruler over his brother. Remember what the name Jacob means? He's living up to it!

Read Genesis 27:30-38. No sooner does Jacob leave his father than in comes Esau who gets the surprise of his life! His brother has been there before him and stolen his blessing! How does Isaac react? (Isaac begins to shake all over.) Esau is upset and very angry. He says Jacob's name fits him! He rails about Jacob taking away his birthright first and now his blessing. He's gotten it all. Esau weeps in frustration begging his father to bless him with *something, anything,* but Isaac basically says, "What's left to give?"

Read Genesis 27:39-40. Isaac blesses him with a prediction that he will not serve his younger brother forever, but will one day throw off that yoke from his neck and be free of it. This is not much of a consolation prize to Esau who remains furious. This is somewhat similar to Cain and Abel. One brother is so jealous and angry that all he can think about is destroying his brother. When we're angry and the temptation to do wrong is strong, we need to remember Cain and Esau and pray that God will help us to control our anger and handle the situation in the right way. Esau, like Cain, will not.

Read Genesis 27:41-45. Esau is so angry he vows to kill Jacob once their father dies. Rebekah hears about his plan and prepares to get Jacob far away to safety to her family living in Haran. Rebekah only intends for Jacob to be gone how long? (A few days) Unfortunately, these "few days" will turn out to be more than twenty years.

Read Genesis 27:46. Rebekah doesn't want to tell Isaac the real reason she's sending Jacob away. Esau is his favorite son and Jacob was wrong in stealing the blessing from him. Perhaps she knows this will just upset her husband further. She comes up with an excuse that she wants Jacob to get a wife from among her relatives because she can't stand the Canaanite women that Esau has married. (This part was true; Rebekah didn't like her daughters-in-law!)

Read Genesis 28:1-5. Isaac accepts Rebekah's story, calls Jacob to him, gives him instructions, and sends him away with another blessing. Whose blessing was it? (The blessing of Abraham) Remember, Jacob is Abraham's grandson. Where was Jacob's destination? (Padan Aram) This was where Rebekah was from and where her family still lived. She and Isaac wanted Jacob to marry one of Laban's daughters. What relation was Laban to Rebekah? (He was her brother.)

Read Genesis 28:6-9. Esau knows his parents don't like his Canaanite wives and that Jacob is obeying them by going away to marry a relative. He tries to please his parents by taking a relative as well. He marries a woman from the family of Ishmael. Remember how Isaac and Ishmael got along and the kind of man that Ishmael was? This probably didn't please Esau's parents as much as he had hoped.

<u>Review Questions:</u>   (Answers are provided in the Answer Key.)

1. How old was Isaac when Jacob and Esau were born?

2. What does Esau mean?

3. What does Jacob mean?

4. What was Esau good at?

5. What did Esau sell to Jacob?

6. What did Isaac want to do before he died?

7. Who came up with the idea to steal the blessing?

8. What animal skin did Rebekah put on the back of Jacob's neck and hands?

9. Why didn't Isaac recognize Jacob?

10. Isaac was confused because the hands were the hands of Esau, but what was Jacob's?

11. Isaac blessed Jacob and then Esau came in. What was Isaac's reaction?

12. What was Esau's reaction when he heard Jacob took his blessing?

13. What did he beg his father to do?

14. Isaac blessed him, but was it as good as Jacob's blessing?

15. What did Esau want to do to Jacob?

16. Who heard about Esau's plan?

17. She told Isaac that Jacob needed to leave to get a wife from her relatives. Did Isaac agree to send Jacob away?

18. Why did Isaac and Rebekah not like Esau's wives?

19. What did Isaac bless Jacob with before he left home?

20. What did Esau do to try to please his parents?

"Putting Down Roots": Memory Work

•   Memorize Genesis 28:3

•   Memorize the meanings of Esau - "hairy" and Jacob - "supplanter" or "heel-grabber"

"Farther Afield": Map Work

Map 4

- Locate the land of Padan Aram
- Locate the country of Syria

 ## "Harvest Fun": Games & Activities

- Jacob or Esau – Each player needs 2 index cards or pieces of paper. One should say "Jacob" and the other "Esau". Let one person be the clue reader. As each clue is read, each player must decide the correct answer and hold up that name card. Be careful, there might be some tricky ones! The player with the most right answers at the end of the game wins.

1. I was a great hunter. (Esau)

2. I was the youngest twin. (Jacob)

3. I was a smooth-skinned man. (Jacob)

4. Rebekah is my mother. (Both!)

5. My name means "hairy". (Esau)

6. I was grabbing my brother's heel at birth. (Jacob)

7. I despised and sold my birthright. (Esau)

8. I was married to Canaanite women. (Esau)

9. I liked to hang out at home. (Jacob)

10. I cooked dinner one day and sold it to my hungry brother. (Jacob)

11. Isaac is my father. (Both!)

12. My name means "supplanter". (Jacob)

13. I was favored by my father. (Esau)

14. My father asked me to hunt for him and fix him some savory food. (Esau)

15. I was favored by my mother. (Jacob)

16. I deceived my father into giving me my brother's blessing. (Jacob)

17. At one time, I wanted to kill my brother. (Esau)

18. I dressed up in my brother's clothes. (Jacob)

19. Abraham is my grandfather. (Both!)

20. I was distraught when I found out my brother stole my blessing. (Esau)

- Identification Game – How many items can you identify using your other senses besides sight? Isaac was deceived by his son, Jacob because he couldn't see. He was confused because he used his senses of hearing, touch, and smell to figure out which son it was. Have one person gather several items and place them in a dark tote bag or pillowcase. Players need to be blindfolded, then reach in the bag and try to identify each item by touching, smelling, or listening to it. See how many each player can identify correctly. Some suggested items to use: comb, small scented candle, baby rattle, pencil, apple, banana, cotton ball, rubber band, cinnamon stick, orange, bell, small book, box of paper clips, click-top pen, crayon, small container of play-doh, a rock, whole cloves, a golf ball, a hair clip, emery board.

"Digging Deeper": Research

- Birthrights – Esau sold his birthright to his brother Jacob for just a pot of stew. He gave up <u>a lot</u>. What all was included with the birthright?

- Family Connections – Isaac and Rebekah were not happy with the Canaanite women Esau had married. To please them, he married Mahalath, a family relation. Research Genesis 28:9 to find out what relation she was to Esau.

- Compare/Contrast – Write down the blessing each son of Isaac received. What were the benefits in each blessing? What were the drawbacks? This will help you to see why Esau was so distraught.

 ## "Food For Thought": Puzzles

- Crossword Puzzle – On the following page is a crossword puzzle with clues and answers related to this lesson. If an answer has more than one word, spaces are included. Answers are provided in the Answer Key.

Across

2　Isaac's wife
6　place Jacob was to get a wife
8　meaning of Jacob's name
10　Jacob said he found meat quickly because ____ brought it to him
12　Esau's wife from Ishmael's family
15　Esau wanted to ____ Jacob
16　Rebekah's brother
17　Jacob liked to dwell in these

Down

1　I was red and hairy at birth
3　Esau sold this for a bowl of stew
4　At birth, Jacob grabbed Esau's ____
5　where Esau's wives were from
7　Esau spent his time doing this
9　Jacob put the skin of this on his neck and hands
11　son that received the blessing
13　meaning of Esau's name
14　Jacob tricked Isaac because he was ____

- Word Scramble - Read the clue, then unscramble the word. Answers are provided in the Answer Key.

1. Meaning of Jacob's name   p l r e s a u p n t   _____

2. Age of Isaac when the twins were born   y x t s i   _____

3. Name of Jacob and Esau's mother   h k r e b a e   _____

4. Meaning of Esau's name   y i h r a   _____

5. What Esau sold to Jacob   t b h r i t g h i r   _____

6. What Jacob took from Esau   g s e l i b s n   _____

7. Esau's wives were from this land   n a a a n c   _____

8. Esau was a skillful one   r u n e h t   _____

9. Jacob and Esau did this as babies   g l s r t u g d e   _____

10. Jacob and Esau's grandfather   m r h b a a a   _____

 ## "Fruits Of Our Labor": Crafts

These aren't crafts for this lesson, but rather creative activities. Enjoy!

- Savory Food - Isaac loved to eat the wild game that Esau hunted. Have you ever tasted wild game like venison, wild turkey, pheasant, rabbit, etc.? If you have an opportunity, find a recipe for a dish using game and help prepare it. If you're not able to obtain wild game, you may substitute something local (like chicken) and make a savory dish with it. (Remember, Rebekah substituted goat!) Savory means salty or spicy, not sweet. Maybe you could try a chicken pot pie or chicken-n-dumplings. Be creative and see if your father loves your savory food! For another option, try making a pot of lentil stew like Jacob cooked for his brother.

- Master of Disguise - Jacob got quite elaborate in his disguise to fool his father. He knew he needed to smell and feel like his brother. Think of a Bible character to dress up like. What kind of clothes would they wear? If they're royalty, you might need some things like jewelry, a crown or a scepter. If you're a shepherd, you might need a staff. How about David who played a stringed instrument? If you're Samson, you'll need some bulging biceps and long hair. Don't forget things like wigs or face paint for beards. Try dressing up for your family and see if they can guess which Bible character you are. (You might have to give clues!) Be creative and have fun!

Lesson 10: Jacob's Family

Text: Genesis 29; 30:1-24; 35:16-18

"Growing In The Word": Lesson Text & Discussion

Read Genesis 29:1-9. Jacob reaches the land of Padan Aram and now tries to locate his mother's family. What man is he looking for? (Laban) This is his mother's brother, or his uncle. As he stops at a well, who should come to water the sheep but Rachel, a shepherdess. If she is the daughter of his mother's brother, what relation is she to him? (Cousin)

Read Genesis 29:10-12. Verse 11 says that Jacob wept. He is not crying because he doesn't like the looks of Rachel, or because he is suddenly homesick; he is weeping for joy because he is thrilled to find a relative. He tells Rachel who he is. What does she do next? (She runs home to tell her father.)

Read Genesis 29:13-15. Jacob is welcomed into the family and starts helping out by working with his uncle, Laban. Jacob is not being paid for the work he's doing so Laban asks what he can give him or do for him.

Read Genesis 29: 16-20. Jacob wants to marry Rachel, Laban's younger daughter. Why doesn't he want to marry Leah, the oldest? (She wasn't very pretty while Rachel is said to be beautiful.) Laban agrees to the marriage, but first...how long must Jacob work for Rachel? (7 years) That seems like a long time, doesn't it? Did Jacob mind? (No, they seemed but a few days to him.)

Read Genesis 29:21-27. The wedding finally happens. A big feast is held and the bride is given, but OOPS! It's the wrong one! Jacob doesn't realize until the next morning that his wife is not Rachel, but Leah! Would you be happy if you were Jacob and you had been tricked like that? He was very angry. He had waited and worked for Rachel for seven years and he didn't even get her. What was Laban's excuse for this? (Laban's excuse was that it was the custom for the oldest to marry first.) He assures Jacob that he can still marry Rachel too, but he's also stuck with Leah. This is a case of "the shoe being on the other foot". Remember how Jacob tricked his father to get something he wanted and it made his brother very angry? Now Jacob is the one who was tricked and he doesn't like it at all when he's the one who was deceived. Ironic, isn't it? You may wonder how Jacob was tricked at all. For one thing, the wedding probably took place in the evening as Jewish weddings would take place at sundown. Also, the brides would be heavily veiled so that it is possible he couldn't see her face at all or not clearly. It is also possible that wine was flowing freely as they celebrated. Laban gives his daughter, Leah a wedding present – her own maid. What is her name? (Zilpah)

Read Genesis 29:28-30. Jacob now marries Rachel too, but has to work for Laban a little longer. How much longer? (7 more years!) Rachel also receives a wedding present from her father, her own maid. What is the maid's name? (Bilhah)

Read Genesis 29:31-35. God sees that Leah is unloved so he blesses her with children while keeping Rachel from having any. Keep in mind that names in the Bible are very significant. Let's look at Leah's first four children and the meanings of their names: Reuben means "sees" (God saw her affliction), Simeon means "hearing" (God heard), Levi means "attached" ("Surely Jacob will now be attached to me after giving him three sons!"), Judah means "praise" ("I will praise the Lord").

Read Genesis 30:1-8. Rachel is more loved than her sister, but she's very unhappy because she has no children. It makes her jealous of Leah. In her anger and frustration, she demands that Jacob give her children. What is his response? ("Am I in the place of God?") Jacob is angry at her in return. He is not God! Only God can bless with children if He chooses. Rachel's solution will seem very familiar...(Remember Sarah and Hagar?) She gives her maid, Bilhah, to Jacob and she has a son named Dan. Dan means "judge". Rachel says that God has judged her case. Bilhah has another son, Naphtali, which means "wrestling". Rachel says she has wrestled with her sister.

Read Genesis 30:9-13. Leah has stopped bearing children so she copies her sister. She gives her maid, Zilpah, to Jacob. Zilpah has a son named Gad which means "troop" because Leah said, "A troop comes". Zilpah has another son, Asher, which means "happy" because Leah said, "I am happy".

Read Genesis 30:14-21. Leah is listened to by God and allowed to bear three more children. Issachar means "my hire". Zebulun means "endowment". Then she gave birth to Jacob's only daughter. What name was given to her? (Dinah)

Read Genesis 30:22-24. God now "remembers" Rachel. Had he forgotten about her all of this time and how desperately she wanted a child? Not at all. When the Bible says that God "remembers" someone, it means He is about to act for their benefit. God now allows Rachel to have the long-awaited child, a son she names Joseph. His name means "God shall add". Rachel now fully expects God to continue to bless her with more children.

Read Genesis 35:16-18. Rachel has a second son, but in the process loses her life. She starts to name him Ben Oni which means "son of my sorrow", but Jacob calls him Benjamin which means "son of my right hand". Jacob now has 13 children in all, 12 sons and 1 daughter.

Review Questions: (Answers are provided in the Answer Key.)

1. What city did Jacob's Uncle Laban live in?
2. What was Rachel's occupation?
3. Which sister was the beautiful one?
4. How long did Jacob agree to work for Laban in order to marry Rachel?
5. Did he mind waiting that long?
6. Whom did Jacob marry first?
7. Why?
8. Who was Leah's maid?
9. Who was Rachel's maid?
10. How many children did Jacob have in all?
11. How many did Leah have and what were their names?

12. Who were Rachel's children?

13. Who were Zilpah's children?

14. Who were Bilhah's children?

15. What happened to Rachel at Benjamin's birth?

 ## "Putting Down Roots": Memory Work

- Memorize the 12 sons of Jacob in birth order: Reuben, Simeon, Levi, Judah, Dan, Naphtali, Gad, Asher, Issachar, Zebulun, Joseph, Benjamin

- Memorize the mothers and which children belong to them: Leah – Reuben, Simeon, Levi, Judah, Issachar, Zebulun, Dinah; Rachel – Joseph, Benjamin; Zilpah – Gad, Asher; Bilhah – Dan, Naphtali

 ## "Farther Afield": Map Work

Map 4

- Trace Jacob's journey from his home in Beersheba to Haran. He stopped at Bethel where he had the dream of the ladder with angels ascending and descending on it. Mark Bethel on your map. Place an angel sticker or drawing of an angel next to it to remind you of Jacob's dream.

 ## "Harvest Fun": Games & Activities

- Guess Who? - Use 12 index cards or pieces of paper. For each card, write 3-4 clues using name meaning, birth order, mother's name, and possibly name of sibling. At the bottom of the card write the answer. Use one card per son of Jacob. After the clues and answers have been written down. Shuffle the twelve cards and lay them face down. Take turns drawing a card and reading the clues to the other players giving clues one at a time until the correct name is guessed.

- Guess Who #2 – Have 2 cards, write "Leah" on one and "Rachel" on the other. Each player needs a set of these cards. Hold up the correct answer to each clue as it is read.

1. I am the oldest sister. (Leah)

2. I was barren for a long time. (Rachel)

3. I was a shepherdess. (Rachel)

4. Jacob is my husband. (Both!)

5. Reuben is my firstborn. (Leah)

6. I was very beautiful. (Rachel)

7. I was married first. (Leah)

8. I am the youngest sister. (Rachel)

9. Jacob loved me most. (Rachel)

10. I had six sons and one daughter. (Leah)

11. My eyes were delicate. (Leah)

12. Zilpah was my maid. (Leah)

13. One of my son's names means "praise". (Leah)

14. My last born son's name means "son of my right hand". (Rachel)

15. I envied my sister because she was having so many children. (Rachel)

16. Bilhah was my maid. (Rachel)

17. Joseph was my oldest. (Rachel)

18. Zebulun was my youngest son. (Leah)

19. Laban was my father. (Both!)

20. I gave my maid to my husband, Jacob. (Both!)

 ## "Digging Deeper": Research

- Life of Jacob – Learn more about Jacob's life while he lived in Haran. Read the rest of Genesis chapter 30 and all of chapter 31. Either answer the following questions or share what you've learned by telling it to someone.

1. How did Jacob get along with his father-in-law, Laban?

2. Did Jacob become rich or poor?

3. What was the reason behind Jacob's success?

4. How many times did Laban change Jacob's wages?

5. What made Jacob decide to leave?

6. Did Laban approve?

7. What did Laban do when he found out?

8. Who kept Laban from harming Jacob?

9. How did they resolve their differences?

10. What did they agree to and how did they part?

*   Biblical Weddings & Feasts – Learn about Jewish weddings and wedding feasts. There are some good books available on everyday life in the Bible and Jewish feasts and customs. What might Jacob's wedding(s) have been like?

 ## "Food For Thought": Puzzles

*   Matching – Match the name to its meaning. Answers are provided in the Answer Key.

Reuben	praise
Simeon	God shall add
Levi	son of my right hand
Judah	God sees
Dan	my hire
Naphtali	a troop comes
Gad	attached
Asher	hearing
Issachar	judge
Zebulun	wrestling
Joseph	endowment
Benjamin	happy

- Word Scramble – Unscramble the names from this lesson. Answers are provided in the Answer Key.

e r c a l h	_____	p o s j e h	_____
m i a e n j n b	_____	n r b e u e	_____
h a l b i h	_____	s a s h c a r i	_____
b a n l a	_____	e n i s m o	_____
n u b e z l u	_____	h p t l a n i a	_____

"Fruits Of Our Labor": Crafts

- Jacob's Family Tree – On a large piece of paper or on poster board, draw Jacob's family tree. You may want to start with Abraham and Sarah at the base of the tree and then go up from there. Include the four women and all of the sons. Don't forget Dinah!

- Your Family Tree – While you're in the practice of making a family tree, why not do one of your own family? See how far back you can trace your ancestors. Learning your family history can be very fascinating and fun! If you have any pictures of your family members, copy them, cut them out, and paste them on the appropriate branches of your tree.

Lesson 11: Joseph's Coat of Many Colors

Text: Genesis 37:1-11

"Growing In The Word": Lesson Text & Discussion

Read Genesis 37:1-2. Jacob and his family are settled in the land of Canaan, the land promised to Jacob's grandfather, Abraham, and his descendants. How old is Joseph at this time? (17) What is he doing and who is he with? (He is tending the flocks with his brothers.) He is not with all of his brothers, but rather, he is with the sons of Bilhah and the sons of Zilpah the two maids. Which brothers would these be? (Dan, Naphtali, Gad, and Asher) Were these sons of Jacob doing a good job at shepherding? (No) Joseph brought back a bad report of them to their father, Jacob.

Read Genesis 37:3. Why did Jacob love Joseph more? (He was the son of his old age.) Joseph was also the son of Rachel, the wife that Jacob loved the most. Was it right for Jacob to show favoritism? (No) How could this cause problems in the family? Jacob gives Joseph a tunic of "many colors". This may not actually refer to a lot of different colors, but it could mean that the coat had long sleeves or was one that was richly decorated. Whatever it was, it was a very special coat and a very special present.

Read Genesis 37:4. Why did his brothers hate Joseph? (They could see that their father loved him more. They were jealous.) If you were in their shoes, would you be jealous too? Would it be hard to be kind to Joseph? Remember Cain & Abel and Jacob & Esau? Jealousy can lead to a bad end if it's not dealt with in the right way. Will Joseph's brothers handle it better than others before them? We will learn more about this later.

Read Genesis 37:5-8. Describe the first dream of Joseph. (He dreamed that as he and his brothers were binding sheaves of wheat in the field, all of their sheaves of wheat bowed down to his sheaf.) What was it about this dream of Joseph's that made his brothers so mad? (The fact that the dream seemed to indicate that they would all bow down to their little brother.) If it isn't bad enough that Joseph gets special treatment, now he's dreaming about his brothers bowing down to him! They are furious!

Read Genesis 37:9-11. Describe Joseph's second dream. (He dreamed that the sun, moon and eleven stars bowed down to him.) Why did his father rebuke or scold him? (He thinks Joseph is going too far in saying his father and mother will bow to him.) His father does wonder what this all means and keeps it in mind. What did his brothers feel about him at this point in time? (They envied him.) Again, they are consumed with jealousy and it is simmering inside them all waiting to reach a boiling point.

Review Questions: (Answers are provided in the Answer Key.)

1. How old is Joseph when he receives his coat from his parents?

2. Why did Jacob love Joseph more than his other children?

3. What kind of coat did Jacob give Joseph?

4. What is another name for this garment?

5. How did Joseph's brothers feel about him?

6. How many dreams did Joseph have?

7. Describe the dreams.

8. What did his father and brothers think that these dreams meant?

9. How did Joseph's brothers feel about him after he told them the dreams?

10. What did his father do when he heard the dreams?

 "Putting Down Roots": Memory Work

• Memorize Genesis 37:3

• Memorize and summarize Joseph's two dreams

 "Farther Afield": Map Work

Map 2

• Refresh your memory as to the land of Canaan and locate some of the following places if you're not familiar with where they are. Since our last lesson, Jacob has lived in Bethel, Ephrath (Bethlehem) and Kirjath Arba (Hebron) where his father Isaac died and was buried. Jacob and his family are now living near the town of Shechem.

• Locate the cities of Ephrath (Bethlehem) and Kirjath Arba (Hebron)

 "Harvest Fun": Games & Activities

• I Spy - Since we're talking about colors this lesson, how about playing a game of "I Spy"? Let one person be "it". They will locate something in the room that everyone can see and then begin by saying, "I spy something that is green (or red or blue, etc.). Others will make guesses as to what the object is. (Maybe it's Mom's green shirt or a green bean or houseplant.) Whoever guesses first correctly gets to be "it" next.

- "Tell a Story" Cards - Joseph was eager to share his dreams with his family. Make cards using items from this lesson such as the sun, moon, stars, grain, coat, etc. or you may use the cards from Lesson 1. Place the cards face down in a pile on the table. Let one player pick a card making sure no one else sees it. He then will tell a Bible story about the item on the card and the other players have to guess what item is on the card. For example, you pick a card with a sun on it. You may tell the story of Joseph's dream about the sun, moon and stars bowing down to him or the story of Joshua commanding the sun to stand still, or the fourth day of creation. The first person to correctly guess the item gets to go next. Another variation of this game is for a player to pick the top card off of the pile and lay it face up on the table for all to see. The player who picked the card will start by telling a Bible story about the item. Then the player to his left has to tell a different Bible story about the same item. The play keeps going around the table until someone can't come up with a Bible story about the item on the card. That person is then "out". The person next to him picks a new card and begins again. Play continues until one person is left. They're the winner!

"Digging Deeper": Research

- Joseph's Coat of Many Colors - Joseph's coat of many colors was a tunic. What was a tunic? What were they made out of? How were they worn? Was the coat actually made up of many colors? What are some other possible meanings?

- Shepherds - What was it like to be a shepherd in Bible times? What would a typical day be like? What would the responsibilities be? Would it be boring, dangerous, or fun? Joseph and his brothers were shepherds and his mother Rachel was a shepherdess as well as his grandmother Rebekah. Can you think of other Bible characters who were shepherds? It was a popular occupation!

 ## "Food For Thought": Puzzles

- Word Search Puzzle – The following page contains a word search puzzle for this lesson. Happy hunting! Answers are provided in the Answer Key.

```
E  S  S  S  E  S  N  M  C  S  T  A  R  S  F
O  E  J  H  W  S  A  N  O  O  M  R  R  E  H
D  Y  A  O  K  O  M  F  A  T  H  E  R  V  P
L  T  C  C  H  B  B  A  B  A  H  C  O  A  E
E  C  O  I  Y  V  N  E  E  T  N  E  V  E  S
I  L  B  N  S  C  O  L  O  R  S  A  R  H  O
F  E  B  U  N  I  A  R  G  S  D  F  C  S  J
V  T  N  T  I  I  B  R  E  I  G  N  F  S  O
```

Jacob	Joseph	brothers	colors
tunic	field	dreams	sheaves
grain	sun	moon	stars
flocks	seventeen	bows	reign
envy	hate	mother	father
Canaan			

- **Coded Message**

__ __ __ __ __   __ __ __ __ __   __ __ __ __ __ __
17 26 24 12 25   15 12 5 22 23   17 12 8 22 11 19

__ __ __ __   __ __ __ __   __ __ __   __ __ __
14 12 9 22   7 19 26 13   26 15 15   19 18 8

__ __ __ __ __   __ __ __ __ __ __ __ __   __ __ __
12 7 19 22 9   24 19 18 15 23 9 22 13   26 13 23

__ __ __ __   __ __ __   __   __ __ __ __ __   __ __
14 26 23 22   19 18 14   26   7 6 13 18 24   12 21

__ __ __ __   __ __ __ __ __ __ .
14 26 13 2   24 12 15 12 9 8

<u>Key to the Code</u>:

J	F	N	R	U	A	G	O	S	V	C	H	T	D	I	E	B	W	K	Y	P	M	L
17	21	13	9	6	26	20	12	8	5	24	19	7	23	18	22	25	4	16	2	11	14	15

 "Fruits Of Our Labor": Crafts

- Diorama - Make a diorama of one of Joseph's dreams. A diorama is a scene in miniature. There are several good books and websites that can show you how to make different kinds of dioramas. You can start with an empty shoe box or a flat piece of wood. You can use a variety of materials to make grass, trees, rocks and even realistic looking water. You can use materials from around the house or you can visit a craft shop to purchase tiny diorama models of things like grass, trees, animals, etc. The point is to use your imagination, be creative, and have fun!

- Sand Painting - Use the coat template found in Appendix B. Make a copy of it on sturdy paper such as card stock. Use a sponge brush to paint a thin layer of glue on the coat. Sprinkle colored sand in designs to make a colorful coat.

Lesson 12: Joseph Sold Into Slavery

Text: Genesis 37:12-36; 39; 40

"Growing In The Word": Lesson Text & Discussion

Read Genesis 37:12-17. Joseph is sent again to check up on his brothers. What are they doing? (Tending the flocks) They're not near home because flocks would need to be moved around to different grazing areas in order to have a continuous supply of food. They could be a few miles from home or a few days' journey. They're not in the location Joseph believes them to be. They have moved on and he finds them near Dothan.

Read Genesis 37:18-24. His brothers see him coming and before he even gets there, they plot to kill him. They are so consumed with jealousy and hate. They even plan a lie to tell their father, covering up their evil deed. How do they refer to Joseph? (The dreamer) They think if they get rid of him, his dreams will die right along with him! Reuben talks them out of killing Joseph, convincing them instead to just throw him in a pit. Why does he suggest this? (He fully intends to rescue Joseph later on and take him home.) As the oldest, he's responsible for the welfare of his younger brother. Older siblings should take note of this - be a protector of your younger siblings! What did they do to Joseph before throwing him into the pit? (They stripped him of his tunic, his special coat.)

Read Genesis 37:25-28. The brothers sit down to eat, then Judah comes up with a brilliant plan - to sell Joseph and make some money off of him! The others like the plan and a band of Ishmaelite merchants conveniently comes by and buys him. How much do they pay for Joseph? (20 shekels of silver) Any guesses as to how much money this would be? Actually, we can't say for sure. We could compare it to what the current value of silver is today which would be around $230, but a lot of it would depend on the weight of each shekel, the purity of the silver, and the value of silver at the time. One of my resources listed it at around $2,500. The point is, poor Joseph's freedom was worth more than any amount of money. His brothers sold it very lightly.

Read Genesis 37:29-30. Apparently, Reuben wasn't around when all of this took place because he returns to find Joseph has been sold and he is distraught to find him gone. What will he tell his father?!?

Read Genesis 37:31-36. To cover their evil deed and commit further sin, the brothers concoct a lie to explain Joseph's disappearance. They kill a goat, dip Joseph's beautiful coat in its blood and show it to their father to let him think that a wild animal killed Joseph. Jacob is beside himself with grief! How would you feel if you were Jacob? What do you think his other sons were thinking as they stood there and watched their father weep and mourn over his lost son? They try to comfort their father, but it is no use. Jacob is overwhelmed with grief. Meanwhile, Joseph is sold in Egypt to a man named Potiphar. What position does he hold? (He is an officer of Pharaoh and a captain of the guard.)

Read Genesis 39:1-6. The Lord is with Joseph and blesses him even in his slavery. Jospeh is made an overseer in Potiphar's house which means he's in charge of everything. Potiphar was very pleased with Joseph and the good work that he did.

*verses 7-16 (This passage is left to your discretion as to whether to cover it now or how to cover it, depending on the ages of your children. It is possible to paraphrase it in a way that conveys the message without being explicit.)

Read Genesis 39:7-16. Potiphar's wife is also pleased with Joseph, but not in the right way. As a married woman, she should love and be faithful to her husband, but instead, she keeps looking longingly at Joseph – a man she cannot rightfully have. She tries to tempt Joseph every chance she gets to "lie with her". This is something that God only permits married people to do with each other. Joseph strongly refuses her temptations. He knows that Potiphar trusts him completely, and he doesn't want to betray him, but that is not the reason he refuses her. Who does Joseph say he doesn't want to sin against? (God) Joseph calls this sin what it is: a great wickedness before God and he refuses to participate in it. Does that stop Potiphar's wife from trying? No! One day, she sees her chance when she finds herself alone in the house with Joseph. She grabs his garment and demands that he lie with her. What does Joseph do? (He leaves the garment in her hand and runs!) Notice he didn't stay there and have a long, drawn-out discussion with her, allowing himself to be more and more tempted. He sees this dangerous situation of temptation for what it is and does the best thing he can – gets away from there as fast as he can! **Read I Corinthians 6:18** and **II Timothy 2:22.**

Read Genesis 39:17-20. Potiphar's wife gets Joseph into some serious trouble - she falsely accuses him and her husband is so angry he has Joseph thrown into prison. If you were Joseph, would you be really discouraged about now? First, he is sold into slavery by his own brothers and doesn't know if he will ever see his family again. Then, he is falsely accused and winds up in an Egyptian prison. However, Joseph doesn't give up on God.

Read Genesis 39:21-23. Even as Joseph's life seems to go from bad to worse, God is in control. He continues to bless Joseph. Joseph is put in charge of all the prisoners and the jailer trusts him completely. Why did Joseph enjoy a measure of success? (God was prospering him in whatever he did.)

Read Genesis 40:1-4. Joseph gets two interesting prisoners entrusted to his care: Pharaoh's chief baker and his cupbearer or butler. Why were they put into prison? (They had done something to offend or make Pharaoh angry.)

Read Genesis 40:5-8. Both of these men had dreams on the same night and wanted someone to interpret them. What does interpret mean? (To tell what something means) Notice who Joseph credits with the interpretation of dreams. (God)

Read Genesis 40:9-15. The cupbearer tells his dream first. Describe his dream. (The cupbearer dreams about a vine with three branches. The branches budded and blossomed and produced ripe grapes. He took the grapes, pressed them into Pharaoh's cup, then handed the cup to Pharaoh.) He gets a good interpretation - in three days he'll be out of prison and back to work serving wine to Pharaoh. What does Joseph ask of him? (He wants the butler to mention him to Pharaoh because he's wrongly imprisoned.)

Read Genesis 40:16-19. The baker is now anxious to hear his interpretation - he's hoping for the same good news, but he won't be so lucky. Describe the baker's dream. (The baker dreamed that he had three white baskets on his head. The top basket had all kinds of baked goods for Pharaoh, but the birds came and ate them out of the basket.) What does Joseph tell him? (In three days, the baker will be executed and the birds will eat his flesh.)

Read Genesis 40:20-23. In three days, Pharaoh had a birthday party; his butler was restored to his place and his baker was hung, just as Joseph interpreted. Sadly though, the butler forgot all about Joseph and he continued to sit in prison, waiting.

Review Questions: (Answers are provided in the Answer Key.)

1. What did Joseph's brothers want to do to him first?

2. Whose idea was it to throw him in a pit?   Why did he suggest this?

3. Whose idea was it to sell him instead?

4. Who bought him and for how much?

5. How did the brothers cover up what they'd done?

6. Was Jacob's family able to comfort him?

7. Whom was Joseph sold to?

8. What position did Joseph hold?

9. Who falsely accused Joseph?

10. Where did Potiphar put Joseph?

11. What position did Joseph have there?

12. What 2 officers of Pharaoh were put in prison?

13. Why were they sad one morning?

14. Who did Joseph say interpretations belong to?

15. Who was to be restored to Pharaoh's court?

16. Who was executed?

17. How many days after Joseph interpreted the dreams did these things happen?

18. Who had a birthday party?

19. Joseph told the cupbearer that he was in prison _____.

20. Who forgot all about Joseph?

 "Putting Down Roots": Memory Work

- Memorize Genesis 39:2

- Memorize Genesis 39:21

- Memorize the dreams of the baker and the butler and the interpretations of them.

"Farther Afield": Map Work

Map 1

- Locate the city of Shechem in the land of Canaan - Joseph's brothers had the flocks here before moving them to Dothan.

- Locate the country of Egypt

- Locate the Nile River - this is the lifeline of Egypt

"Harvest Fun": Games & Activities

- "Stay Out of that Pit!" - Use the game board in the templates of Appendix B. Photocopy the two game board pages and tape them together or glue them onto something sturdier such as poster board or cardboard. Use a die to determine the number of spaces to move and use buttons or small game pieces for markers. Questions to be used can be the review questions and memory work from this lesson or for more of a challenge, use review questions from previous lessons. If you land on a square with a star, you must answer a question. If you answer correctly, you get another turn. If you give the wrong answer, you must "sit in the pit" for an extra turn. If you land on a "sit in the pit" space, you must also go there for an extra turn and then you may resume the space you were on. Whoever reaches the finish square in Egypt first wins.

- Who Am I? - Guess the people from this lesson using the clues given. This may be played in two teams or award points to individuals who guess first. Higher points could be awarded the earlier the correct guess is given. Answers are provided in the Answer Key.

1. Clue #1) I am captain of Pharaoh's guard. Clue #2) I have a wicked wife. Clue #3) I bought Joseph as a slave but had him put in prison.

2. Clue #1) I am one of Jacob's sons. Clue #2) I didn't like Joseph, but I didn't want to kill him. Clue #3) I was going to get Joseph out of the pit later when no one was around.

3. Clue #1) I am an officer of Pharaoh's court. Clue #2) I had a dream in prison. Clue #3) I was hanged from a tree.

4. Clue #1) I am a shepherd. Clue #2) I gave my favorite son a special coat. Clue #3) I was distraught thinking my son was dead.

5. Clue #1) I have 11 brothers. Clue #2) I was tending my father's flocks when Joseph came along. Clue #3) It was my idea to sell Joseph.

6. Clue #1) I am one of Jacob's sons. Clue #2) God blessed my work. Clue #3) I was sold into slavery.

7. Clue #1) I am an officer in Pharaoh's court. Clue #2) Joseph interpreted my dream. Clue #3) I was let out of prison and restored to Pharaoh's court.

8. Clue #1) We ride camels. Clue #2) We are traders and merchants. Clue #3) We bought Joseph for 20 shekels of silver.

9. Clue #1) I live in Egypt. Clue #2) I accused Joseph wrongfully. Clue #3) Joseph wouldn't do what I wanted.

10. Clue #1) I live in Egypt. Clue #2) I became angry with some of my officers. Clue #3) I had a birthday party.

"Digging Deeper": Research

- Hebrews - Notice that Joseph is referred to as a "Hebrew". The Jews were also known as Hebrews throughout the Bible. Where does this name come from?

- Egyptian Culture - Joseph would have entered a very different culture than what he was used to when he lived in Canaan. Read some books on what life was like in Ancient Egypt. Note specifically how slaves were treated.

"Food For Thought": Puzzles

- Crossword Puzzle – The following page contains a crossword puzzle for this lesson. Answers are provided in the Answer Key.

Across

4 It was his idea to sell Joseph
8 Joseph was taken here after being falsely accused
9 This brother didn't want to kill Joseph
10 Where Joseph found his brothers with the flocks
11 What the officers of Pharaoh had while in prison
12 The number of days it would be for the dreams to come true
14 Joseph's first position as a slave

Down

1 Joseph said interpretations of dreams belong to ___
2 This officer of Pharaoh would be hanged
3 Number of shekels Joseph was sold for
5 Jacob thought a wild _____ had killed his son
6 The baker and ___ had offended Pharaoh and were put in prison
7 The officer restored to court didn't _____ Joseph
8 Pharaoh's captain of the guard
13 This animal's blood was put on Joseph's coat

• Word Search - Answers are provided in the Answer Key.

```
D S E T I L E A M H S I E N R L E
T R E B M E M E R E Y H R C U I D
P E A H R A E T N R K N E E H S R
Y H H H C O U I E M O H K K P V E
G T A V P N V V C S G R A P E S A
E O F R I I A N I A P D B C S L M
U R A C A L T R E C I F F O O C S
B B R T S O P O B U T L E R J T M
J E A E P L H E P P L E P S E I E
```

Joseph	dreams	brothers	pit
slavery	Ishmaelites	Egypt	Potiphar
Pharaoh	officer	prison	tunic
goat	butler	baker	vines
branches	grapes	cup	shekels
remember			

 "Fruits Of Our Labor": Crafts

• Storyboard - Take a piece of poster board and divide it (draw) into 6 squares. Draw the story of Joseph being sold into slavery one square at a time: Square 1 - Joseph finds his brothers tending the flocks. Square 2 - They throw Joseph into a pit. Square 3 - They sell him to the Ishmaelite traders. Square 4 - They put goat's blood on the coat. Square 5 - They show the coat to Jacob who cries. Square 6 - Joseph arrives in Egypt where Potiphar buys him. Drawing can be difficult, especially people, so another option would be to find some free printable pictures off of the Internet that you could color yourself and cut out. When your storyboard is complete, show it to someone and tell the story to them.

- Act it Out! - Act out the scene in the prison where Joseph interprets the dreams of the baker and the butler. You will need three people to dress in costumes and be Joseph, the baker, and the butler. If you'd like, record it on video. Be sure to make a creative scenic background of the prison. During the scene, have the baker and butler waking up and being miserable about the night they just had with these strange dreams. Joseph will come in and ask what's wrong. They will tell him and Joseph will give credit to God for interpretations. Then they'll each tell him their dream and Joseph will tell them what's going to happen. How will the butler react to the news? How will the baker react?

Lesson 13: Joseph in Egypt

Text: Genesis 41; 42; 43; 44; 45; 47; 50

 ## "Growing In The Word": Lesson Text & Discussion

*This is a long lesson covering seven chapters. This portion of the lesson may take two or three days to cover.

Read Genesis 41:1-8. When we last left Joseph, he was still in prison, waiting. When this chapter opens, how many years has he continued to be in prison? (2) Describe the two dreams of Pharaoh. (The first dream was about 7 cows coming up out of the river that were big and fat followed by 7 other cows that were ugly and very thin. The thin cows ate up the fat cows. The second dream was about 7 heads of grain that were plump and good being devoured by 7 scraggly, thin heads of grain.)

Read Genesis 41:9-13. Who *finally* remembers Joseph to Pharaoh? (The chief butler) When he hears Pharaoh talking about dreams, the light bulb goes off in his head and he tells Pharaoh all about Joseph and how he interpreted his own dream when he was in prison.

Read Genesis 41:14-32. Joseph is sent for immediately. What is done to him before he can appear before Pharaoh? (He is shaved and his clothes are changed.) Pharaoh tells Joseph that he's heard that he can understand dreams and their meanings. How does Joseph respond to that? (He gives credit to God.) Joseph then explains to Pharaoh what his dreams mean. What is God showing him? (There will be seven years of plenty of food followed by seven years of famine.) What is a famine? A famine is an extreme shortage of food. 7 years would be a very long time to have a food shortage, wouldn't it?

Read Genesis 41:33-36. What advice does Joseph give to Pharaoh? (He says Pharaoh should appoint a wise man as a ruler to supervise gathering 1/5 of the produce of the land during the plentiful years and then store it up as a food reserve for the years of famine.)

Read Genesis 41:37-46. Does Pharaoh think this is good advice? (Yes) He appoints Joseph as the ruler and puts him second in command of all Egypt under only Pharaoh himself. He gives Joseph several things. What are they? (His signet ring, garments of fine linen, a gold chain around his neck, a new name, and a wife.) What was the name Pharaoh gave to Joseph? (Zaphnath-Paaneah) What was the name of Joseph's wife? (Asenath) How old was Joseph when this all took place? (30 years old) Do you remember how old Joseph was when he received his special coat? (17) Thirteen years have now gone by!

Read Genesis 41:47-57. Joseph puts his plan into action and it works! The extra grain was stored up in the years of plenty and when the years of famine began, people from other countries started coming to Egypt to buy food. During this time, Joseph and his wife have two sons. The firstborn is Manasseh whose name means "forget" for Joseph said, "*God has made me forget all my toil and my father's house*". His second son was named Ephraim whose name means "fruitful" for Joseph said, "*God has caused me to be fruitful in the land of my affliction*".

Read Genesis 42:1-5. The famine has reached the land of Canaan as well. Jacob sends 10 of his sons to Egypt to buy grain. Who had to stay home and why? (Benjamin - Jacob wants to keep him home where he's protected from any harm. Jacob thinks Benjamin is the only living son left of Rachel, and he's not about to let anything happen to him.)

Read Genesis 42:6-17. Joseph recognizes his brothers at once, but they don't recognize him! Why do you think this is? (It has been over 20 years since they've seen him and Joseph is probably dressed in the manner of the Egyptians. Not to mention the fact that since they sold their brother into slavery, they would *never* expect to see him as the second in command of all Egypt.) Seeing his brothers bowing to him reminded Joseph of something; what was it? (His dreams) How does he speak to his brothers and why do you think that is? (He speaks roughly or harshly. He's probably upset at the sight of them as it would bring back the unpleasant memories of what they had done to him.) What does Joseph accuse them of? (Being spies) How long does he put them in prison? (3 days)

Read Genesis 42:18-26. Joseph brings them out of prison and tells them what they must do: one brother has to stay behind in prison while the others can return home with the food for their families. He also asks them to bring something back to him. What was it? (Their youngest brother, Benjamin) The brothers have an interesting conversation right in front of Joseph who understands their language. They think he's just some Egyptian ruler who wouldn't understand the Hebrew language at all so they speak freely to each other. In verses 21 and 22, what do they say is the reason all of this misfortune is falling upon them? (They think this is all happening because of their evil deed toward Joseph. They think that now they are being punished for what they've done years ago.) Which brother basically says, "I told you so!" (Reuben) How does this conversation affect Joseph? (He weeps.) He turns away so they don't see him crying, but he is very affected by what he has just heard. What command does Joseph give concerning the money his brothers have paid for the grain? (He has it placed back in their grain sacks.) Which brother is left behind in prison? (Simeon)

Read Genesis 42:27-29. Tragedy! When they encamp and start to feed their animals, they find their money in their sacks! What must be going through their minds? They know at some point they have to return to Egypt to get Simeon out of prison. It's possible they will be accused of theft and be in real trouble! They still believe that God is punishing them. They continue home to their father and tell him everything that has happened. What they *won't* tell him is that they think all of these bad things are God's punishment for selling Joseph. Their sin of selling Joseph and covering it up has not just "gone away". God doesn't forget about sin, no matter how much time passes.

Read Genesis 42:30-35. (This is just a retelling of the events previously read.)

Read Genesis 42:36-38. What is Jacob's reaction to all of this news? (He's very upset.) Jacob thinks Joseph is long dead, now Simeon is in an Egyptian prison and they want to take Benjamin to Egypt where something might happen to him. Reuben says a very interesting thing to his father. What is it? (He says Jacob can kill Reuben's two sons if Reuben doesn't bring Benjamin back home safely.) Jacob would certainly never do this. The point Reuben is strongly making is that he will do whatever it takes to bring Benjamin back home. There is **no way** he is going to let anything bad happen to Benjamin. He is taking full responsibility for him. Do you think he's feeling a guilty conscience over Joseph? If Benjamin were lost to Jacob under Reuben's protection, he offers the lives of not one of his sons, but *two*. It's as if he's indicating that he's responsible for the lives of both Joseph and Benjamin. Despite any reassurance from Reuben, Jacob is determined that Benjamin will stay home.

Read Genesis 43:1-15. The brothers stay home in Canaan until it is absolutely necessary to return to Egypt. They're running out of food again. Why have they waited so long to return? (They know they have to take Benjamin with them in order to see the ruler (Joseph) again. Also, there is still the issue of the money in their sacks.) Another brother now speaks up to take personal responsibility for Benjamin. Which one is it? (Judah) Jacob reluctantly agrees to let

Benjamin go. He has no choice; they will starve otherwise. What does he send with them this time? (Double the money and some presents for the man in charge.)

Read Genesis 43:16-23. They appear with Benjamin before Joseph. They are then all taken to Joseph's house for a meal. Why do they think they're being taken there? (They think they are in trouble and will face punishment over the money in their sacks.) What explanation is given to them by Joseph's steward about the money? (He said it was their God blessing them with money.) Simeon is then released.

Read Genesis 43:24-30. As the brothers enter Joseph's house, what does the steward do for them? (He gives them water to wash their feet and feeds their donkeys.) As they are brought before Joseph, they bow down to him again. Who does Joseph ask them about? (Their father) He surely longs to see him again and wants news of his health and well-being. What is Joseph's reaction to seeing his brother, Benjamin, after so many years? (He has to leave the room quickly to weep.) Benjamin was probably just a young child the last time Joseph saw him over twenty years earlier.

Read Genesis 43:31-34. Why were the Egyptians and Hebrews seated at separate tables? (It was an abomination to the Egyptians. Hebrews were shepherds and were looked down on by Egyptians who were very clean-shaven and hygienic.) The brothers are amazed to see themselves seated in the order of their birth. How did this happen? (Joseph knew their birth order and had them seated that way.)

Read Genesis 44:1-2. What does Joseph command to be placed in Benjamin's sack? (His silver cup) Why do you think he does this? (Joseph is testing them to see how they will handle this situation when Benjamin is found to be the "guilty" one.) He also commands their money to be placed in their sacks again.

Read Genesis 44:3-9. They're barely out of the city when Joseph's men come after them, accusing them of stealing his silver cup. The brothers, of course, have no idea about the cup and foolishly say that if it's found in any of their sacks, that man will die and the rest of them will be slaves. This is how sure they are of their innocence. However, we should learn a lesson from this to *think* before we speak. The brothers will learn this lesson too late.

Read Genesis 44:10-13. Notice that Joseph's steward doesn't agree to their terms, but rather says the guilty one only will be a slave and the rest can go free. Again, remember that Joseph wants to see if his brothers will try to save Benjamin or if they're willing to sacrifice him like they did Joseph years ago. When the cup is discovered in Benjamin's sack, what is the reaction of his brothers? (They tear their clothes.) This is a sign of great sorrow and distress. This is the very thing their father Jacob had feared – that something would happen to Benjamin.

Read Genesis 44:14-34. They all return to the city to again appear before Joseph. Judah confesses that God is punishing them, but doesn't say for what. He makes a desperate plea to spare Benjamin. He goes so far as to offer *himself* as a slave so that Benjamin can safely return home to their father. My, how things have changed! Remember, it was Judah's bright idea (and wish) to sell Joseph as a slave. I think he feels quite differently now. Whose feelings is he now considering that he didn't seem to care about before? (His father's) What does Judah say will happen to his father if they return home without Benjamin? (He will die from the grief.) Judah is willing to do anything to keep that from happening.

Read Genesis 45:1-8. The time has come at last! Joseph reveals himself to his brothers. He first sends everyone else out of the room, then makes his dramatic announcement, "I am

Joseph!" Wouldn't you love to have been a fly on the wall at that moment? Can you imagine the looks on his brothers' faces? What thoughts must have run through their heads! What is their reaction? (They're dismayed! They can't even speak, at first.) Joseph doesn't want to punish them; he wants them to all be a family again. He doesn't blame them for selling him into slavery. In fact, he says three times that it was someone else who was responsible for him being in Egypt. Who was it? (God)

Read Genesis 45:9-20. Joseph gives instructions and supplies for them all to go home and move the entire family to Egypt where Joseph can look after them. The famine is not over yet. How many more years does Joseph say it will last? (5) After Joseph talks with them, he kisses his brothers and weeps over them. He is truly happy to be reunited with his family. Who hears about Joseph's family reunion? (Pharaoh) Pharaoh is also glad about this for Joseph's sake. What does Pharaoh offer to do for Joseph's family? (He sends carts from Egypt to Canaan so that all of the family and little ones can ride back to Egypt in them. He also offers some of the best land for them to live in and the best food of the land for them to eat. They will be treated like royalty.)

Read Genesis 45:21-28. They go home and tell their father the news. Can you imagine how Jacob must have felt when he heard it? At first, Jacob doesn't believe it. The Bible says, *"His heart stood still."* After believing Joseph to be dead for over twenty years, it would certainly be heart-stopping to be told he is alive. Jacob can hardly believe it's true, but he sees all of the things Joseph has sent back and realizes that it *is* true. He is anxious to go and see his son. Each brother had also been given new clothes. What did Benjamin receive? (300 pieces of silver and five new garments) How many donkeys had been sent to Jacob and what were they loaded with? (10 male donkeys were loaded with good things from Egypt, 10 female donkeys were loaded with food and provisions for the journey to Egypt.)

Read Genesis 47:1-12. Joseph's family is now situated in Egypt in the land of Goshen, some of the best land there is. It is located in the Nile Delta which is well-watered and fertile. When Joseph presented five of his brothers before Pharaoh, what offer did Pharaoh make them? (He offered to make any qualified men among them chief herdsmen of his own livestock.) Joseph also brings his father before Pharaoh. What did Jacob do to him? (He blessed him.) Pharaoh asked Jacob how old he was. What was his answer? (130 years)

Read Genesis 47:13-26. This takes us through the last five years of the famine and how the people were provided for. At first, the people paid money for the stored-up grain, but eventually, the money ran out. What did the people use next to pay for their grain? (They used their animals.) This lasted for about a year and then the people ran out of animals to use to buy their grain. The next thing the people offered in exchange for their grain was the land that they owned. The land became Pharaoh's and the people moved off of their land and into the cities. The last thing Joseph does is to put a tax on the people of 1/5 of their harvest. When crops started growing again, the people promised to pay 1/5 of the harvest to Pharaoh and keep 4/5 for themselves.

Read Genesis 47:27-31. How many years did Jacob live in Egypt? (17 years) Jacob is now about to die and wants Joseph to bury him with his family in the land of Canaan. How old is Jacob? (147)

Read Genesis 50:1-14. Jacob dies, is mummified and taken for burial to Canaan as he wished. Where was the burial site? (The cave in the field of Machpelah) Abraham bought this as a family burial plot years before. **Read Genesis 23** to find out who he bought it from and how much he paid for it. How many days did the embalming/mummification process take? (40 days) How many days did the Egyptians mourn for Jacob? (70 days) There was a large group of family and friends that traveled to Canaan to bury Jacob. How many days of mourning took place in the land of Canaan? (7 days) They mourned so greatly that the Canaanites noticed it and called the name of the place "Abel Mizraim." Can you guess what that name might mean? (It means the "mourning of Egypt".)

Read Genesis 50:15-21. Now that Dad's gone...What are the brothers afraid of? (Joseph may now take revenge on them.) What is Joseph's reaction to this? (He's upset.) He only wants to take care of them and treat them with kindness. He tells them again that this was all *God's* will. He doesn't want them to be afraid. He assures them that he wants to take care of them and their families. How did he speak to them? (He spoke kindly.) As tempting as it could have been to take vengeance, Joseph chose to forgive and love. He did not choose the path of repaying evil for evil, but instead overcame evil with good. **Read Romans 12:17-21.**

Read Genesis 50:22-26. Joesph dies and is mummified. How old was he? (110) What request did he make before he died? (He requested that his bones be taken out of Egypt when the Israelites leave at God's calling one day to go back to Canaan for good.) This will be fulfilled over 400 years later when Moses leads the Israelites out of Egypt in the Exodus.

Review Questions: (Answers are provided in the Answer Key.)

1. While Joseph remained in prison, who finally remembered him to Pharaoh?
2. When Pharaoh told Joseph he had heard Joseph could give the meaning of dreams, to whom did Joseph give credit?
3. How many years of plenty were there going to be in Egypt?
4. What would those years be followed by?
5. What was Joseph's advice to Pharaoh?
6. How old was Joseph when Pharaoh made him second in command of all of Egypt?
7. Who was Joseph's wife?
8. When Joseph's brothers came to Egypt to buy grain, how long had it been since they had seen him?
9. Why did his brothers not recognize him?
10. What did Joseph accuse his brothers of being?
11. Which brother was left home with Jacob and why?
12. Which brother was kept in prison as the others returned to Canaan with the grain they had purchased in Egypt?
13. What had Joseph commanded be put in the grain sacks of his brothers before they returned home?
14. As the brothers returned to Egypt a second time to buy grain, who did they have

to bring with them by order of Joseph?

15. Which brother promised Jacob that he would protect his younger brother at all costs?

16. How did Joseph react to seeing his brother, Benjamin?

17. How were the brothers seated in the house of Joseph and why?

18. As all of the brothers prepared to return home once again, what did Joseph command to be placed in Benjamin's grain sack?

19. What test is Joseph giving his brothers by doing this?

20. Why do the brothers think all of these bad things are happening to them?

21. When the brothers are brought before Joseph with the "stolen" silver cup, which brother offers himself as a slave in place of Benjamin?

22. What was the first reaction of the brothers when Joseph revealed himself to them?

23. Joseph did not blame his brothers for what they had done to him. Why did he say it had happened?

24. At this point in time, how much longer did Joseph say the famine would last?

25. Each brother was given new clothes by Joseph, but what did Benjamin receive?

26. What part of Egypt did Joseph's family settle in?

27. How old was Jacob when he died?

28. Where was Jacob buried?

29. How old was Joseph when he died?

30. What command did Joseph give concerning his bones?

 "Putting Down Roots": Memory Work

- Memorize Pharaoh's two dreams and their interpretations.

- Memorize Genesis 50:24

- Memorize Romans 12:21

"Farther Afield": Map Work

Map 3

- Locate the Nile Delta

- Locate the land of Goshen - This is the land Pharaoh gave to Joseph's family to shepherd their flocks. Would this have been considered prime real estate? Why or why not?

 "Harvest Fun": Games & Activities

- Find Joseph's Cup - Joseph had his silver cup hidden in Benjamin's sack of grain. Take a fancy silver cup or a special cup from your kitchen or purchase an inexpensive silver one from a dollar store or party supply store. Take turns hiding the cup somewhere in the house. Then let the other players find it. You may tell them "hot" or "cold" the closer or farther away they get from the hiding place. After you play, review why Joseph hid his cup.

- Field trip - Visit a museum that has Egyptian artifacts on display or a mummy exhibit.

 "Digging Deeper": Research

- Egyptian Mummification - Both Jacob and Joseph were mummified. Research the process of mummification. An excellent resource to use is a book called *Mummies Made in Egypt* by Aliki. It is available from most libraries.

- Famines - For most of this lesson, there was a severe famine affecting Egypt and surrounding countries. Research the effects of famine in ancient cultures. What steps would people take to deal with the effects?

"Food For Thought": Puzzles

- Fun with Hieroglyphics - Hieroglyphics is the picture and symbol language the ancient Egyptians used. In Appendix B you will find a hieroglyphics chart. Use this for the following activities: 1) Write your name in hieroglyphics. 2) Write a message in hieroglyphics and let someone decode it using the chart. 3) Let someone make a message for you in hieroglyphics for you to decode. 4) Look up Joseph's Egyptian name and write it in hieroglyphics. Ask someone to guess what Bible character it is.

"Fruits Of Our Labor": Crafts

- Build a Pyramid - Use sugar cubes and glue or frosting to stick them together in the form of a pyramid. The great pyramids of Egypt had probably already been built by the time Joseph was there. It's quite possible even Abraham saw them when he was in Egypt years earlier! A good resource book about pyramids and how they were built is *Pyramid* by David Macaulay.

- Beaded Jewelry - The Egyptians liked to look good! They usually wore white linen clothing. Both men and women wore jewelry, but not just for decoration. It was also a symbol of their status or they wore charms that they believed were lucky. Things such as bracelets, rings, earrings, and beaded collars were made from gold, precious stones, and beads of glass or stone. Try making some beaded jewelry. Get some beads or a bead-making kit from a craft store. To make a simple bracelet, use some thin elastic string (comes on a spool) and measure a length of it around your wrist. Allow some extra for tying it off; it can always be trimmed. String some beads on it then tie a square knot. It will be stretchy to fit over your hand and onto your wrist. Read up on different methods of beaded jewelry making and experiment. Have fun!

Answer
Key

ANSWER KEY

Lesson 1:

Review Questions:

1. Who was in the beginning before creation? (God)

2. What five elements do we see in the very first verse of the Bible? (Time, Force, Energy, Space, and Matter)

3. What did God create on each of the seven days? (Day 1 – light, Day 2 – firmament or air we breathe, Day 3 – dry land and green things, Day 4 – sun, moon and stars, Day 5 – fish and fowl, Day 6 – man, woman and all land animals, Day 7 – He rested)

4. What does it mean for plants, trees, and animals to bring forth "after their own kind"? (Apple trees make apples, potato plants make potatoes, birds have baby birds, etc.)

5. What were some of the reasons God made the sun, moon and stars? (Light, day/night, signs/seasons, days/years)

6. Who are the "3 persons" of God? (God the Father, God the Son, God the Holy Spirit)

7. After everything was created, how did God describe it? (Very good)

8. What did God give man authority over? (All living things on the earth)

9. What watered the earth when there was no rain? (A mist)

10. What did God make man out of? (Dust)

11. Did God create dinosaurs? (Yes!) Did they live with man? (Yes!) How do we know? (They were both created on day six.)

12. Describe the creation of man. (God formed man out of the dust of the ground and breathed the breath of life into him.)

13. Described the creation of the woman. (God made Adam fall into a deep sleep, then He opened up Adam's side and removed one of his ribs. God closed up Adam's side, then formed woman from the rib taken from Adam.)

14. What 4 rivers flowed out of the garden of Eden? (Pishon, Gihon, Hiddekel, Euphrates)

15. What one tree was forbidden to man by God? (The tree of the knowledge of good and evil)

- Word Scramble - beginning, heaven, man, rested, mist, dust

Lesson 2:

Review Questions:

1. Who was the serpent? (Satan)

2. What is Satan the father of? (Lies)

3. How many trees were Adam and Eve not allowed to eat of? (One)

4. What was it called? (Tree of the Knowledge of Good and Evil)

5. What lie did Satan tell Eve regarding eating the fruit? (You shall <u>not</u> die.)

6. What three temptations did Eve give in to? (Lust of the flesh, lust of the eyes and the pride of life)

7. What did Adam and Eve try to sew together to make clothes? (Fig leaves)

8. Whom did they try to hide from? (God)

9. Whom did Adam blame? (Eve)

10. Whom did Eve blame? (The serpent)

11. How was the serpent cursed? (Cursed above all animals, crawl on its belly, eat dust)

12. What is the "mother promise" of the Bible? (Genesis 3:15)

13. Whom does Genesis 3:15 prophecy about? (Jesus Christ)

14. How was the woman cursed? (Pain in childbirth, husband will rule over her)

15. How was the man cursed? (Hard labor and sweat to bring forth food from the ground, physical death [dust to dust])

16. What does "Eve" mean? (Mother of all living)

17. From what did God make clothes for Adam and Eve? (Animal skins)

18. What tree did God not want Adam and Eve to eat of after they'd sinned? (Tree of life)

19. What did God do to keep them from returning to Eden and eating of this tree? (Placed a cherubim with a flaming sword at the east side of the garden)

20. What kind of fruit did Adam and Eve eat? (This is a trick question! The truth is, we don't know! The Bible doesn't say what kind of fruit it was.)

- Word Search -

- Matching - Eve-mother of all living, serpent-deceiver, Eden-garden, cherubim-angel, covering-fig leaves, Christ-redeemer, Adam-sweating farmer, garden guard-flaming sword, heel bruiser-Satan, garden walker-Lord

Lesson 3:

Review Questions:

1. Who was Adam and Eve's firstborn? (Cain)

2. What did his name mean? (Gotten or acquired)

3. Who was their second born son? (Abel)

4. What job did Abel have? (Shepherd)

5. What job did Cain have? (Farmer)

6. What did Cain bring as an offering? (The fruit of the ground)

7. What did Abel bring as an offering? (A lamb from the flock)

8. Whose offering was accepted and why? (Abel's; Heb. 11:4 says he offered it by faith)

9. What was Cain's reaction? (He was angry.)

10. What did God warn Cain would lie at his door if he didn't do right? (Sin)

11. What did *Cain* do to Abel? (Murdered him)

12. When *God* asked *Cain* where Abel was, what did *Cain* do? (Lied)

13. What did *God* say cried out to him from the ground? (Abel's blood)

14. What was Cain's punishment? (Great difficulty farming, banishment)

15. Did Cain take his punishment well? (No)

16. What was he afraid someone would do to him? (Kill him for revenge)

17. How did God prevent that? (He put a mark on Cain.)

18. Where did Cain go? (The land of Nod)

19. Who was his first son? (Enoch)

20. Who took two wives? (Lamech)

21. Who was the father of tent-dwellers? (Jabal)

22. Who was the father of musicians? (Jubal)

23. Who was an instructor of every craftsman in bronze and iron? (Tubal-Cain)

24. Who was another murderer besides Cain? (Lamech)

25. Who was the third son of Adam and Eve? (Seth)

- Who Am I?/What Am I? - 1) sheep/lamb, 2) Abel, 3) blood, 4) Adam, 5) earth/ground, 6) Cain, 7) sacrifice/offerings, 8) Eve, 9) sin, 10) fugitive

- Crossword Puzzle -

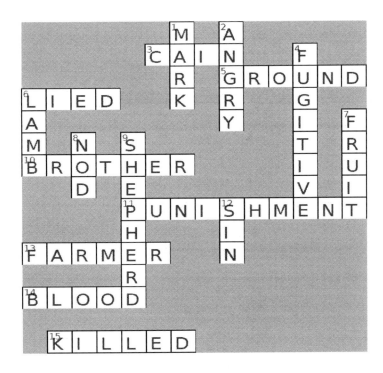

Lesson 4:

Review Questions:

1. How many years warning did God give mankind before He sent the flood? (120)

2. Noah is called a preacher of what? (Righteousness)

3. How bad was man's wickedness? (He thought evil continually.)

4. What did God say He would destroy? (Both man and beast, all living creatures)

5. Noah found _____ in the eyes of the Lord. (grace)

6. How does the Bible describe Noah? (Just, blameless, righteous, perfect in his generations)

7. Who were Noah's sons? (Shem, Ham and Japheth)

8. What was the earth filled with? (Violence and corruption)

9. What was the ark made of? (Gopherwood)

10. What was it covered with inside and out? (Pitch)

11. What were the dimensions (measurements) of the ark? (300 cubits by 50 cubits by 30 cubits)

12. How many windows and doors were there? (One window and one door)

13. How many decks or stories were there? (3)

14. Whom did God establish His covenant with? (Noah)

15. How many people were saved in the ark? (8)

16. How many of each kind of animal were taken into the ark? (2 each, male and female, of the unclean animals; 7 each, male and female, of the clean animals)

17. What else was Noah to take into the ark? (Food for their provisions)

18. How many days after Noah and his family and the animals went into the ark did the flood come? (7)

19. How old was Noah when the flood began? (600)

20. How much of God's commands did Noah obey? (ALL)

- Research #1 -

1. Adam -   Man

2. Seth -   appointed

3. Enosh -   mortal

4. Cainan -   sorrow

5. Mahaleel -   Praise of God

6. Jared -   shall come down

7. Enoch -   teaching

8. Methusaleh -   His death shall bring

9. Lamech -   the lowly, despairing

10. Noah -   rest, comfort

Man appointed mortal sorrow/Praise of God shall come down teaching/His death shall bring the lowly, despairing rest, comfort (Isn't that so neat?!?)

- Animal Matching Puzzle #1 - bull-male alligator, sow-female pig, jenny-female donkey, drake-male duck, doe-female deer, tom-male turkey, jill-female kangaroo, gander-male goose, buck-male deer, vixen-female fox, rooster-male chicken, nanny-female goat, mare-female horse

- Animal Matching Puzzle #2 - colt-baby horse, joey-baby kangaroo, calf-baby whale, tadpole-baby frog, cygnet-baby swan, pup-baby shark, hatchling-baby alligator, kit-baby skunk, fawn-baby deer, shoat-baby pig, cub-baby panda, kid-baby goat, gosling-baby goose, chick-baby bird

Lesson 5:

Review Questions:

1. How old was Noah when the flood began? (600)

2. How long did it rain? (40 days and 40 nights)

3. What were the two sources of water? (Rain from the heavens, fountains of the great deep)

4. Who shut the door of the ark? (God)

5. How many days did the waters prevail on the earth? (150)

6. When and where did the ark rest? (17th day of the 7th month on the mountains of Ararat)

7. What two kinds of birds did Noah send out? (Raven and dove)

8. Which one returned? (dove)

9. Why did Noah wait to leave the ark? (He was waiting for God's permission/instructions)

10. When did they leave the ark? (601st year of Noah's life, 27th day of the 2nd month)

11. How long were they in the ark altogether? (1 year and 10 days)

12. When they came out, was the ground soggy and muddy or completely dry? (Completely dry)

13. What was the first thing Noah did? (Built an altar and sacrificed to God)

14. What did God now give permission for man to eat? (Meat)

15. What was man not allowed to eat and why? (Blood, life is in the blood)

16. God now institutes capital punishment or the death penalty for killing someone. What is the reason given? (Man is made in the image of God.)

17. What is a covenant? (An agreement between two parties)

18. God made a covenant with whom? (Noah and all future generations of people)

19. What did God promise? (Never to destroy the earth again with a worldwide flood)

20. What was the sign of the covenant? (Rainbow)

- Word Scramble - rain, animals, fountains, dove, rainbow, forty, wind, raven, sacrifice, covenant

- Numbers Matching -

  600- age of Noah at the beginning of the flood
  7- number of clean animals
  2- number of pairs of unclean animals
  40- days and nights of rain
  150- number of days water stood on the earth
  7- number of days Noah waited before sending out the dove
  3- number of Noah's sons
  8- number of people saved on the ark
  300- length of ark in cubits
  15- number of cubits the waters prevailed above the mountains
  17- day of the month the ark rested on the mountains of Ararat

Lesson 6:

Review Questions:

1. At the beginning of this lesson, how many languages were there? (One)

2. Where did the people settle? (The land of Shinar)

3. What building materials did they use? (Bricks that they made and asphalt or bitumen for mortar)

4. What did they want to build? (A tower to reach the heavens and a city)

5. For what reason? (1. To make a name for themselves, 2. To stay in one place)

6. Who came down to see the work? (God)

7. What did God propose to do to stop the work? (Confuse their language)

8. Once He did this and they couldn't understand each other, what did God do? (Dispersed, or scattered, them over the face of the earth)

9. What is the name given to that place? (Babel)

10. Why is it called that? (It is where God confused their language.)

• Word Search Puzzle -

Lesson 7:

Review Questions:

1. Who called Abraham to leave his home country? (God)

2. What were the three promises God made to Abraham? (1. Great nation, 2. Land of Canaan, 3. All families of earth blessed through him.)

3. How old was Abraham when he left his home? (75)

4. Who was Sarah's maid? (Hagar)

5. What country was she from? (Egypt)

6. What did Sarah do when she thought she couldn't have children? (Gave Hagar, her maid, to Abraham as another wife)

7. Was this a good idea? (No) Why or why not? (It went against God's plan.)

8. Who was Hagar's son born to Abraham? (Ishmael)

9. How old was Abraham when his first son was born? (86)

10. Who was the "son of promise" born to Sarah and Abraham? (Isaac)

11. What does his name mean? (Laughter)

12. How old was Abraham when he was born? (100)

13. Did the two brothers get along? (No)

14. Where did Ishmael go to grow up? (Wilderness of Paran)

15. What country was his wife from? (Egypt)

• Who Am I? - 1) Lot, 2) Hagar, 3) Sarah, 4) Ishmael, 5) Abraham, 6) Isaac, 7) the Angel of the Lord

• Crossword Puzzle -

Lesson 8:

Review Questions:

1. Who tested Abraham? (God)

2. Where was Abraham to take Isaac and what was he to do with him? (Land of Moriah, offer him as a sacrifice)

3. How many days did they travel? (3)

4. Who did Abraham say would come back? (We, meaning himself and Isaac)

5. What New Testament scripture tells us what Abraham thought would happen? (Hebrews 11:17-19)

6. What question did Isaac ask his father? ("Where is the lamb?")

7. What was Abraham's reply? ("God will provide the lamb.")

8. Who stopped Abraham? (The Angel of the Lord)

9. What did God provide in place of Isaac? (A ram)

10. What did Abraham call the place and what did it mean? (Jehovah Jireh, the Lord will provide)

- Coded Message – Abraham said it to his son, Isaac.

- Word Search Puzzle -

Lesson 9:

Review Questions:

1. How old was Isaac when Jacob and Esau were born? (60)

2. What does Esau mean? (Hairy)

3. What does Jacob mean? (Supplanter or heel-grabber)

4. What was Esau good at? (Hunting)

5. What did Esau sell to Jacob? (His birthright)

6. What did Isaac want to do before he died? (Eat some savory game that Esau had hunted and prepared)

7. Who came up with the idea to steal the blessing? (Rebekah)

8. What animal skin did Rebekah put on the back of Jacob's neck and hands? (Goatskin)

9. Why didn't Isaac recognize Jacob? (He was blind.)

10. Isaac was confused because the hands were the hands of Esau, but what was Jacob's? (The voice)

11. Isaac blessed Jacob and then Esau came in. What was Isaac's reaction? ("He trembled exceedingly", he was shaking like a leaf!)

12. What was Esau's reaction when he heard Jacob took his blessing? (He was angry and crying.)

13. What did he beg his father to do? (Bless him too)

14. Isaac blessed him, but was it as good as Jacob's blessing? (No)

15. What did Esau want to do to Jacob? (Kill him)

16. Who heard about Esau's plan? (Rebekah)

17. She told Isaac that Jacob needed to leave to get a wife from her relatives. Did Isaac agree to send Jacob away? (Yes)

18. Why did Isaac and Rebekah not like Esau's wives? (They were Canaanite women.)

19. What did Isaac bless Jacob with before he left home? (Abraham's blessing)

20. What did Esau do to try to please his parents? (Married Ishmael's daughter)

- Word Scramble - 1) supplanter, 2) sixty, 3) Rebekah, 4) hairy, 5) birthright, 6) blessing, 7) Canaan, 8) hunter, 9) struggled, 10) Abraham

• Crossword Puzzle -

Lesson 10:

Review Questions:

1. What city did Jacob's Uncle Laban live in? (Haran)

2. What was Rachel's occupation? (Shepherdess)

3. Which sister was the beautiful one? (Rachel)

4. How long did Jacob agree to work for Laban in order to marry Rachel? (7 years)

5. Did he mind waiting that long? (No)

6. Whom did Jacob marry first? (Leah)

7. Why? (Laban tricked him.)

8. Who was Leah's maid? (Zilpah)

9. Who was Rachel's maid? (Bilhah)

10. How many children did Jacob have in all? (13)

11. How many did Leah have and what were their names? (7 – Reuben, Simeon, Levi, Judah, Issachar, Zebulun, Dinah)

12. Who were Rachel's children? (Joseph and Benjamin)

13. Who were Zilpah's children? (Gad and Asher)

14. Who were Bilhah's children? (Dan and Naphtali)

15. What happened to Rachel at Benjamin's birth? (She died.)

• Matching – Match the name to its meaning. Answers are in the Answer Key.

Reuben- God sees
Simeon- hearing
Levi- attached
Judah- praise
Dan- judge
Naphtali- wrestling
Gad- a troop comes
Asher- happy
Issachar- my hire
Zebulun- endowment
Joseph- God shall add
Benjamin- son of my right hand

• Word Scramble – Rachel, Benjamin, Bilhah, Laban, Zebulun, Joseph, Reuben, Issachar, Simeon, Naphtali

Lesson 11:

Review Questions:

1. How old is Joseph when he receives his coat from his parents? (17)

2. Why did Jacob love Joseph more than his other children? (He was the son of his old age.)

3. What kind of coat did Jacob give Joseph? (One of many colors)

4. What is another name for this garment? (Tunic)

5. How did Joseph's brothers feel about him? (They hated him.)

6. How many dreams did Joseph have? (2)

7. Describe the dreams. (1. 11 sheaves of grain bowed down to Joseph's sheaf. 2. Sun, moon and 11 stars bowed down to him.)

8. What did his father and brothers think that these dreams meant? (That Joseph would reign or rule over them and they would bow to him.)

9. How did Joseph's brothers feel about him after he told them the dreams? (They hated him even more and envied him.)

10. What did his father do when he heard the dreams? (Scolded or rebuked him)

• Word Search Puzzle -

Lesson 12:

Review Questions:

1. What did Joseph's brothers want to do to him first? (Kill him)

2. Whose idea was it to throw him in a pit? (Reuben) Why did he suggest this? (He intended to come back later and get him out to take him back to their father.)

3. Whose idea was it to sell him instead? (Judah)

4. Who buys him and for how much? (Ishmaelite traders bought him for 20 shekels of silver.)

5. How did the brothers cover up what they'd done? (They killed a goat and dipped Joseph's coat in the blood to let their father think a wild animal had killed him.)

6. Was Jacob's family able to comfort him? (No)

7. Whom was Joseph sold to? (Potiphar)

8. What position did Joseph hold? (Overseer)

9. Who falsely accused Joseph? (Potiphar's wife)

10. Where did Potiphar put Joseph? (Prison)

11. What position did Joseph have there? (He was put in charge of all prisoners.)

12. What 2 officers of Pharaoh were put in prison? (Chief baker and cupbearer)

13. Why were they sad one morning? (They had both dreamed and had no one to interpret the meanings.)

14. Who did Joseph say interpretations belong to? (God)

15. Who was to be restored to Pharaoh's court? (The cupbearer or butler)

16. Who was executed? (The baker)

17. How many days after Joseph interpreted the dreams did these things happen? (3)

18. Who had a birthday party? (Pharaoh)

19. Joseph told the cupbearer that he was in prison _____. (Wrongfully)

20. Who forgot all about Joseph? (The cupbearer)

•   Crossword Puzzle -

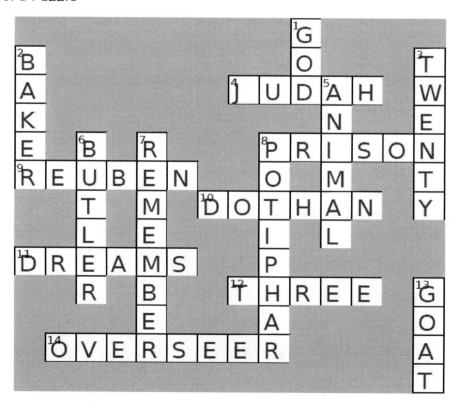

• Word Search Puzzle -

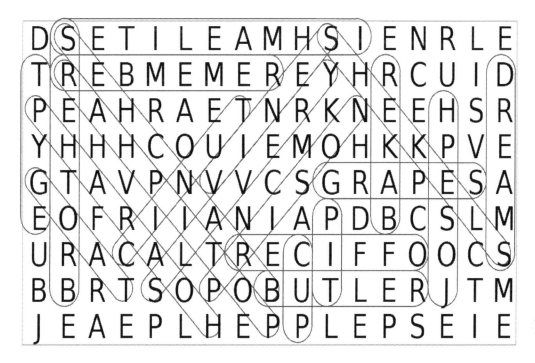

Lesson 13:

Review Questions:

1. While Joseph remained in prison, who finally remembered him to Pharaoh? (The chief butler)

2. When Pharaoh told Joseph he had heard Joseph could give the meaning of dreams, to whom did Joseph give credit? (God)

3. How many years of plenty were there going to be in Egypt? (7)

4. What would those years be followed by? (Seven years of famine)

5. What was Joseph's advice to Pharaoh? (He told Pharaoh to appoint a wise ruler to set apart a portion of the nation's grain during the years of plenty in order to have a food supply during the years of famine.)

6. How old was Joseph when Pharaoh made him second in command of all of Egypt? (30)

7. Who was Joseph's wife? (Asenath)

8. When Joseph's brothers came to Egypt to buy grain, how long had it been since they had seen him? (Over 20 years)

9. Why did his brothers not recognize him? (It had been over twenty years since they had seen him and he was probably dressed like and looked like an Egyptian.)

10. What did Joseph accuse his brothers of being? (Spies)

11. Which brother was left home with Jacob and why? (Benjamin – Jacob would not allow him to go because he didn't want anything to happen to him.)

12. Which brother was kept in prison as the others returned to Canaan with the grain they had purchased in Egypt? (Simeon)

13. What had Joseph commanded be put in the grain sacks of his brothers before they returned home? (The money they had brought to purchase the grain.)

14. As the brothers return to Egypt a second time to buy grain, who do they have to bring with them by order of Joseph? (Benjamin)

15. Which brother promises Jacob that he will protect his younger brother at all costs? (Reuben)

16. How did Joseph react to seeing his brother, Benjamin? (He had to leave the room to weep.)

17. How were the brothers seated in the house of Joseph and why? (Joseph knew their birth order and had them seated that way.)

18. As all of the brothers prepared to return home once again, what did Joseph command to be placed in Benjamin's grain sack? (His silver cup)

19. What test is Joseph giving his brothers by doing this? (He wants to see how far his brothers will go to save Benjamin or if they will treat him as they treated Joseph so many years before.)

20. Why do the brothers think all of these bad things are happening to them? (They think God is punishing them for what they did to Joseph long ago. They feel guilty.)

21. When the brothers are brought before Joseph with the "stolen" silver cup, which brother offers himself as a slave in place of Benjamin? (Judah)

22. What was the first reaction of the brothers when Joseph revealed himself to them? (They were dismayed and couldn't even speak.)

23. Joseph did not blame his brothers for what they had done to him. Why did he say it had happened? (It was God's will for Joseph to come to Egypt.)

24. At this point in time, how much longer did Joseph say the famine would last? (5 years)

25. Each brother was given new clothes by Joseph, but what did Benjamin receive? (300 pieces of silver and 5 new garments)

26. What part of Egypt did Joseph's family settle in? (The land of Goshen)

27. How old was Jacob when he died? (147)

28. Where was Jacob buried? (In the cave in the field of Machpelah which Abraham had bought as a family burial site years before.)

29. How old was Joseph when he died? (110)

30. What command did Joseph give concerning his bones? (He commanded that his bones be taken out of Egypt when the Israelites went back to the land of Canaan for good.)

Appendix A - Maps

Map 1 – Egypt, Canaan and Mesopotamia

Map 2 – Canaan

Map 3 – Egypt, Sinai Peninsula

Map 4 – Syria, Canaan

Map 5 – SE Europe, Middle East, North Africa

*Each item may be photocopied for personal home use as much as needed.

Map 1 - Egypt, Canaan, Mesopotamia

Map should be turned 90 degrees clockwise for proper orientation.

Map 2 - Canaan

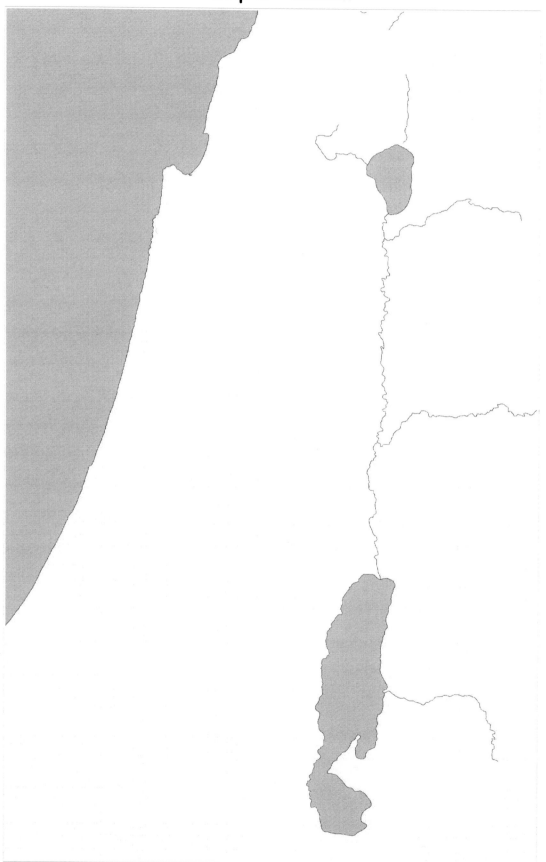

Map 3 - Egypt, Sinai Peninsula

Map 4 - Syria, Canaan

Map 5 – SE Europe, Middle East, North Africa

Appendix B - Templates & Other

Lesson 1 – Creation Cards (Cards may also be used in some subsequent lessons for other activities.)

Lesson 7 – Star template

Lesson 11 – Coat template

Lesson 12 – Game board template

Lesson 13 – Hieroglyphics Chart

*Each item may be photocopied for personal home use as much as needed.

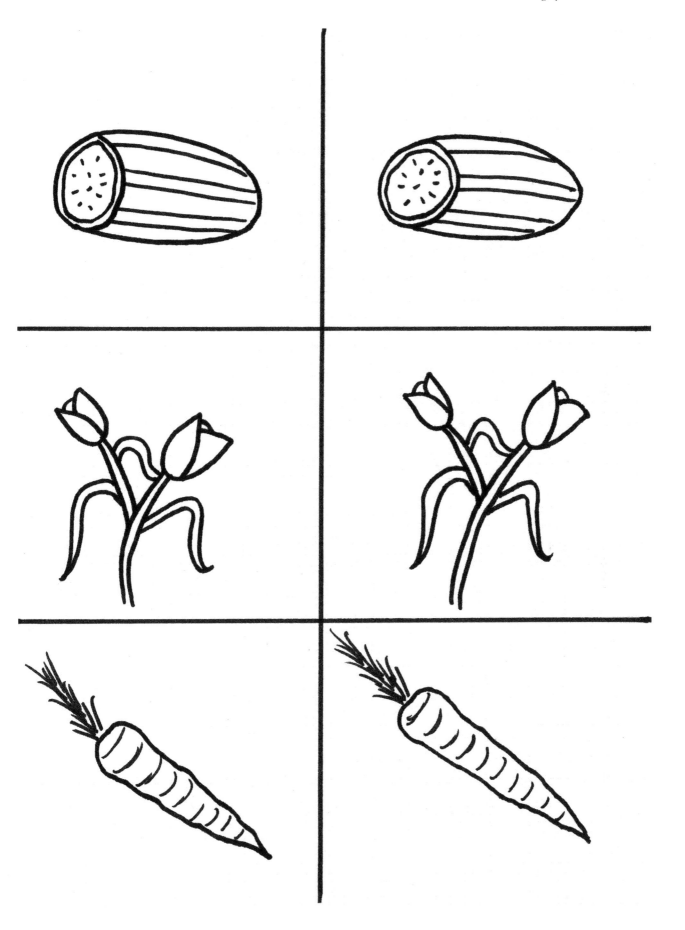

Lesson 7 – Star template

Lesson 11 – Coat template

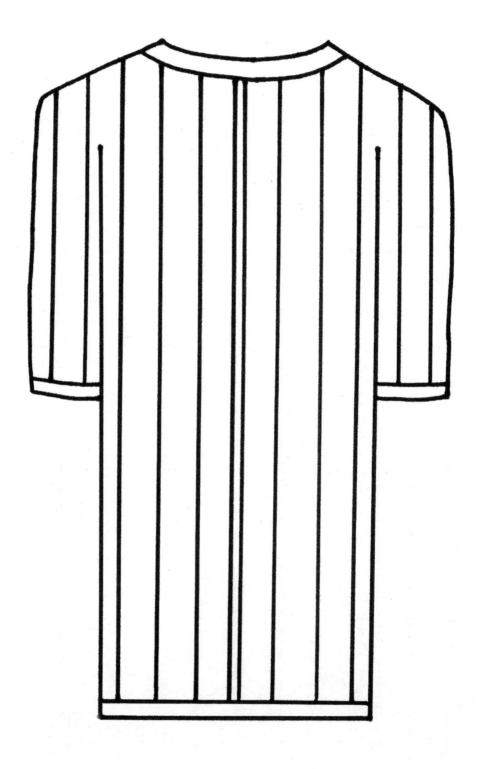

Lesson 12 – Game board template

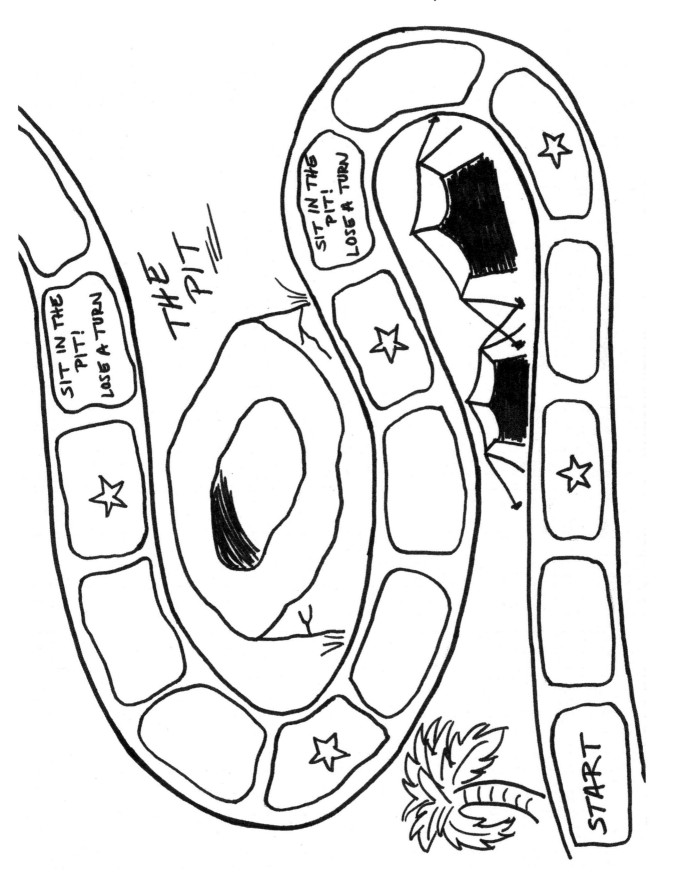

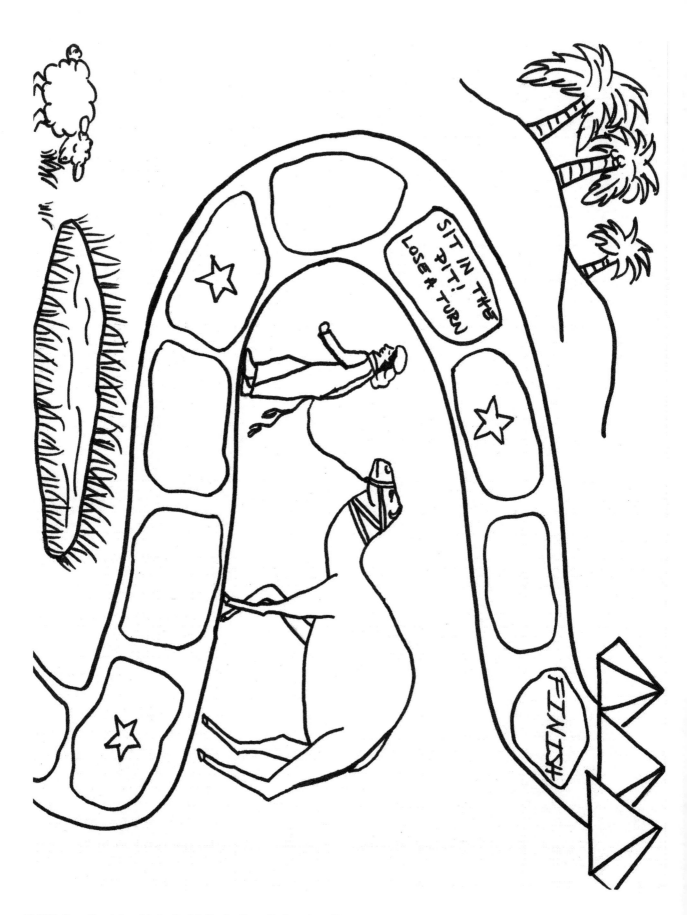

Lesson 13 – Hieroglyphics Chart

Egyptian

Letter	Symbol	Name
A		Vulture
B		Foot
C		Basket
D		Hand
E		Two reeds
F		Viper
G		Cobra
H		Rope
I		One reed
J		Three reeds
K		Hillside
L		Mouth
M		Owl

Hieroglyphics

Letter	Symbol	Name
N		Water
O		Quail chick
P		Stool
Q		Forearm
R		Hobble rope
S		Folded cloth
T		Bread loaf
U		Pot stand
V		Shelter
W		Lake
X		Cow's belly
Y		Unknown
Z		Door bolt

Made in the USA
Middletown, DE
22 October 2016